380110 50 26139 8

FAINT HARPS AND SILVER VOICES

highland
LiBraries

2 2 JUN 2009

25 JUN 2009
- 2 DEC 2010
1 1 JAN 2019
2 1 MAY 2024

D1438111

Other translations by Christopher Middleton

POETRY

Modern German Poetry, 1910–60 (co-editor with Michael Hamburger), 1962
Georg Trakl, *Selected Poems* (editor and contributing translator), 1967
German Writing Today (editor and contributing translator), 1967
Selected Poems of Friedrich Hölderlin and Eduard Mörike, 1972
Selected Poems of Goethe (editor and contributing translator), 1983
Lars Gustafsson, *The Stillness of the World before Bach: New Selected Poems* (editor and contributing translator), 1988
Andalusian Poems (with Leticia Garza-Falcón), 1993

PROSE

Robert Walser, *The Walk and Other Stories*, 1957
Robert Walser, *Jakob von Gunten*, 1969
Friedrich Nietzsche, *Selected Letters*, 1969
Christa Wolf, *The Quest for Christa T.*, 1970
Elias Canetti, *Kafka's Other Trial*, 1974
Robert Walser, *Selected Stories*, 1983 (editor and contributing translator), 1983
Christoph Meckel, *The Figure on the Boundary Line: Selected Prose* (editor and contributing translator), 1983
Gert Hofmann, *The Spectacle at the Tower*, 1984; *Our Conquest*, 1985; *The Parable of the Blind*, 1987; *Balzac's Horse and Other Stories*, 1988

Christopher Middleton

FAINT HARPS AND SILVER VOICES

Selected Translations

SCOTTISH POETRY LIBRARY
5 Crichton's Close
Edinburgh EH8 8DT
Tel. 0131 557 2876

CARCANET

First published in 2000 by
Carcanet Press Limited
4th Floor, Conavon Court
12-16 Blackfriars Street
Manchester M3 5BQ

This selection © Christopher Middleton 2000
The Acknowledgements on pp. 245–246 constitute
an extension of this copyright page

The right of Christopher Middleton to be identified
as the translator of this work has been asserted
by him in accordance with the Copyright,
Designs and Patents Act of 1988

A CIP catalogue record for this book
is available from the British Library
ISBN 1 85754 355 6

The publisher acknowledges financial assistance
from the Arts Council of England

Set in 10pt Garamond Simoncini by Bryan Williamson, Frome
Printed and bound in England by SRP Ltd, Exeter

We must have imagination, awakened by the uncertainty of being able to attain our object, to create a goal which hides our other goal from us, and by substituting for sensual pleasures the idea of penetrating into a life prevents us from recognizing that pleasure, from tasting its true savour, from restricting it to its own range.

There must be, between us and the fish which, if we saw it for the first time cooked and served on a table, would not appear worth the endless trouble, craft and stratagem that are necessary if we are to catch it, interposed, during our afternoons with the rod, the ripple to whose surface come wavering, without our quite knowing what we intend to do with them, the burnished gleam of flesh, the indefiniteness of a form, in the fluidity of a transparent and flowing azure.

Marcel Proust, *Within a Budding Grove*, II,
translated by C.K. Scott- Moncrieff,
London (Chatto and Windus), p.133.

Contents

7

3. ART AND ARTIFICE

4. HUMAN FIGURES

5. FABLED FIGURES

6. THRESHOLDS

9

7. FIRST AND LAST THINGS

Introduction

To begin with, let me explain that this book is meant to be useful. I wanted it to be an aid to inquiry, as well as a source of pleasure. Certainly it is something like a museum, but a museum that is informal, not monumental. If the metaphor be allowed at all, the museum houses culture-specific treasures (the texts grouped under seven headings), and it displays them in perspectives conducive to cross-cultural thinking. So perhaps the book might do service as an aid to 'multicultural' studies. Even if such studies do relate to values that permeate or deregulate different semiotic systems, and even if they are pursued in the thick of intercultural struggles, they ignore at their peril the pivotal rôle of language in the formation of cultures. Here I mean language as the arch-construct of human voices, a mobile construct, of which the veritable poem is a sovereign instance.

Over the years I have been drawn to poems in various languages, and now I have arranged, as it were in seven rooms, some of my translations of those poems. The reader can wander around in those rooms, discovering poems of memory, of love, of the fabulous, and so forth, at his or her pleasure, but also finding useful signposts. The signposts might bring the reader at least to the brink of this or that poet's work, in its own time and through to the present. My fond wish was that intrinsically interesting translations might initiate, sustain, even enrich attention to this or that original work. As for the range of periods and language represented, you can find, for instance, gaps notwithstanding, in the room captioned 'Art and Artifice', translations from German, Swedish, Turkish, French, and Arabic via Spanish, dating from the eleventh century to the 1990s.

But is the selection a bookish rearguard action in the face of changes affecting educational practices now? Heaven knows, the schools and universities do not regulate poetry – the writing and the enjoyment of it. But if, in the universities, free-ranging literary studies are to be replaced by rather more generally 'cultural' or topically 'multicultural' studies, then histories, novels, and plays will yield more grist to the academic mill, and poetry, requiring too much time, will be axed. The study of poetry for its own sake may be doomed, or become at least, in the new noetic ecology, one more endangered species. If that calamity is in store – coupled with a banalizing of poetry in public estimation, its marketing as entertainment – then my metaphor of a museum dissolves into another one; the book becomes a cemetery.

Such a prospect only brightens when we behold the cemetery as a mysterious cavern, like that of the Seven Sleepers, in the hollows and layers of a hill at Ephesus. For when the twilight of literal-mindedness diffused by 'cultural' studies has brought their morning round again, the seven Ephesian topers (as Yeats called them) will fling off their shrouds and quit the tomb. 'Always look on the bright side of death,' quoth Monty Python.

My small museum has internal spaces enough, the luminous and airy spaces of poetic imagination, to house the old alongside the new, as well as some rare poems. Far beyond the reverie of a solitary reader, some poems do disconcert the instruments of power, by decongealing its linguistic codes; at least they resist inertia, dispel the agony of habit, and voice perennial feeling and intelligence about values. A reader will find his or her own perennials here, some even which invoke the *Harmonia Mundi*. Long before Hölderlin wrote his famous line about the poets inaugurating what abides, Hesiod told that utterance from the Muses commemorates 'carefully kept custom-laws' and 'folk-ways'.[1]

Hesiod was, of course, a 'pre-literate' poet, a poet of 'orality'; yet violent mutations in recent poetics and in literacy have not entirely invalidated the ancient basis. There are poets since Goethe, represented in this museum, who harken to the Muses loyally. One of them is the systematic text-artificer Oskar Pastior (b.1927), an 'oral' poet if ever there was one. But his imaginary words, revised 'Crimean Gothic' or otherwise phonetic, as well as the fierce or funny sound-poems of Ernst Jandl, do have to be heard in the original: I found no way to translate them.

*

In this introduction I will not be taking issue with theories about the translation of poems; I want only to address two aspects of this selection which impinge on current debates. The two aspects are: (1) my practice of observing, generally and to the best of my ability, the prosody of the original poem; and (2) certain considerations which led me to organize this selection in seven sets, according to theme.

Especially older poems call for fidelity to form. Obviously a translation of a poem is not replicative like a brass rubbing. Nor is it a performance as in music, even though it will imply an interpretation. The encounter of two languages in a translator's mind will induce mutations in his own language sensibility. Transpositions are negotiated, cultural gaps bridged (or swum) as resources of the host language are mobilized to accommodate its guest. Least of all is translation a fancy way to augment the chatter of the world.

So to the matter of prosody. Meter, rhyme, stanza, caesura, and so forth, in poems from older Western tradition are functions of a poem's whole sense, as tellingly so as are its lexical elements, its 'content'. How a poem speaks, and how it develops, are measures of the significant value in what it says. Over and over again this plain fact has to be stated afresh; thus Seamus Heaney in his 1995 Nobel Prize address – 'truthfulness becomes recognizable as a ring of truth within the medium itself'.[2] Culturally as well as individually the practised sensibility of older poets was attuned to precise prosodic mandates, attuned to a fine degree that can now, perhaps, hardly be matched. The formal movement of words, accomplished as pattern and eliminating (or subduing) all random elements, imbued words with spirit. The poem, it was thought, invited a listener to participate, with heart and mind, if only for a moment, in the dance of transfiguration that life was all about.

It was while looking into prosody of the past – elegiac couplets by Goethe, Hölderlin, and Mörike, for instance – that I realized how false any arbitrary deviation from the original truth-to-tone, or any ignorant mishearing of it, must inevitably be. In the same address, Heaney tells of 'energy released by linguistic fission and fusion . . . buoyancy generated by cadence and tone and rhyme and stanza'. Even in minutely particular terms of how older poets observed the verse-line as such, 'energy' and 'buoyancy' are no empty words: they are just right and they strike home. For older poets (Greek, Latin, Langue d'Oc) the body of the line, levitated in their hearing, sought and in its last syllable found a distinct contour for its mass. The caesura in the second hexameter of an elegiac couplet had its position: if its timing were off, then that second hexameter would not be, as it were, the yoni for the lingam of the first.

If it is absurd to expect such givens of an older poetics to be both translatable and appreciable nowadays, then wait a moment. Well and good, absurd it may be, but I made every effort to avoid bookishness. Translation entails a transposition, on which Haroldo de Campos has bestowed the title of 'transcreation'. Pound's *Cathay* would be a shining example. In transcreation, the entire original 'form' of a poem may be dismantled, or radically modified. Yet even when deviating from the original prosody I have gone neither that way, nor the easier way of 'imitation'. Hölderlin's later poems, which I was translating in 1970–1, seduced me into risking an alternative format, with indented and broken lines (prompted by Hölderlin's own ideas about *harte Fügung*, or rough linking). More recently, Mallarmé's *terza rima* in 'The Jinx', since I could never have got the lines to rhyme in a credible way, called for no less drastic a transposition – the hatching of two shorter lines out of the middle alexandrine, deregulation of the flanking alexandrines, and wandering rhyme or assonance. Fidelity or deviation – all for 'energy', 'buoyancy', and 'the ring of truth'? All, I would prefer to say, for the hearing of the poem's original voice, or voices, even in the foreign English tongue. It is this matter of hearing that seldom figures, oddly enough, in present or past debates about the essentially vocal genre of *lyric*. If the tonal texture of a poem is altogether lost in translation, or if it is not supplied by *anaphony*, then almost everything is lost. Such has often been the case with translations of Rilke into English.

Then one is bound to recognize that, for all that one thought one might have heard, the reader (or listener) hears one's own voice, one's own version of the original voice. Translation is a species of mime, and as the mime embodies another being, the translator envoices other voices in his own tonal scale. The Poundian transcreation is unmistakeably Ezra Pound in 1915. Edward FitzGerald is not Omar Khayyam. It might be suspected that the mimic transcreator (perhaps too the errant imitator) adopts a dominative approach to the original. Even if that is so, translating can serve to restore voices that speak across silences in time. Reaching back through time, or discovering contemporaries, a translator can hear the alien as kin. How inaccessibly 'stylized' Goethe's 'Euphrosyne' might seem, when first you read it. But you go into the text, you tease out of yourself a faculty for hearing the nuances, you catch twisted rays of splendour and untwist them, you come out with a version which you hope has inculcated into English some of the dawdling majesty, some of the heart-throb of Brahms' *Tragic Overture*, even a note or two from Britten's *War Requiem*, for into your perception of the original you have brought your tonal repertory, the archive of your hearing. Finally, even then, your version has to become so instrumented that it delivers the original with as much transparency as possible. You want to transmit the distant voices, past or present. You learn to respect the silences in time, as diners at a Roman banquet respected the command for *silentium* before tucking in: the *silentium* made present 'the glowing world of the ancestors'.[3]

*

It happened that, once I had selected those translations, done over a period of forty years or more, which I felt still held good, I could discern seven areas of thematic emphasis. Though I hesitate to call those areas grossly 'thematic', and prefer to consider them as loose clusters of motifs, within them strange affinities and rifts began at once to manifest themselves between translations from different epochs and languages. It hardly need be noted that no poem (or translation) fits into any sort of 'thematic' slot. 'The Conversation Continues' by Günter Eich, master of sceptical obliquity, could have been included in the Memory area, Rilke's Unicorn sonnet, the one from the second Orpheus cycle, in the area of Fabled Figures, Mallarmé's Swan sonnet in the Thresholds area. Poems in different areas may also answer or question one another. Günter Eich's 'Ryoanji' gainsays certain motifs in Hölderlin's 'Andenken' – traces of the latter, involuntary reminiscences of it, might have stolen across Eich's mind as he composed his own abstrusely allusive text.

Having decided on the seven areas, I then avoided strict chronological sequences and felt free to juxtapose ancients and moderns, strangers and neighbours. I was trusting that the unmistakeable note of each poem would resist any tendency to dissolve into those of its neighbouring poems. I aimed to assemble mosaics that would pronounce a manifold of voices, and, on a limited scale, articulate the polyphony that poems condense out of the 'conversation of mankind'. To enlarge on this briefly: Hölderlin's oft-disputed gnomic conclusion to 'Andenken' – 'Was bleibet aber stiften die Dichter' – can be read as an appeal to the polyphony, to 'tradition'. In the teeth of his catastrophic times, he was claiming not that this or that single poet 'ordains what abides', but that the *poets*, calling to one another across fluctuations of time, are links in what Fabre-d'Olivet, in his great Pythagoras preamble of 1813, was to call 'the golden chain'.[4] The poets, Hölderlin concludes, inaugurate and, as links in a golden chain, stewards in the web of being, sustain self-renewing paradigms, in exemplary song or 'master narrative'. These paradigms penetrate like aquifers the underground galleries of history, or (more benignly, more subtly by far) imagination's pursuit of values in the toils of common existence, in the most volatile nuances of individual experience. 'This we know,' said Chief Seattl in his speech to the US President in 1854, 'the earth does not belong to man; man belongs to the earth. This we know. All things are connected like the blood which unites one family.' Hölderlin's later poems (1801–5) are, in that sense, soaring Greco-Christian geomantic celebrations hatched from an old belief in the primacy of the poetic word. Read as such, the enigmas of 'Patmos' enshrine the wonder and

15

anxiety that inspired it: 'Earth, / Our mother, we have served, and / Latest of all have served / Unwittingly the sunlight . . .'

Ultimately, this is not an anthology of paradigmatic poems, and it does not have a didactic slant. I only translated poems when they intrigued me passionately, held my curiosity, invited response to a challenge. Only from Goethe, Hölderlin, Mörike, and the Arabo-Andalusians did I translate whole clusters of poems. So there was always an aleatory factor at play in the making and selecting of translations, even in the eventual grouping in the seven 'rooms'. I can only hope that a fairly seasoned critical judgement, as well as sheer delight in risking all, conspired with chance to make this book, with its manifold voices, festive and useful.

*

I acknowledge with deep gratitude the help I have received from friends and colleagues. Only during the past six years have I seriously attempted to translate from languages unknown to me, and then only as long as I could work with help from connoisseurs. That work is entirely different in character from the kind that pretends to improve on existing translations without intimate knowledge of the original language or of the original poet's ways of transforming it. In the early 1960s Rafael Nadal urged me to translate with him García Lorca's 'Tamar y Amnon'. The version we came up with was revised in 1986 in collaboration with Leticia Garza-Falcón, together with whom I subsequently translated Arabic poets of Andalusia, from Spanish versions, mostly by Emilio García Gomez, some by Teresa Garulo. Magda al-Nowaihi provided a literal English version of Ibn Khafaja's 'Mountain Poem', and Salma Jayyusi monitored my English transcreation. The poems by Lars Gustafsson were translated in close collaboration with him, directly from Swedish, sometimes aided by Verena Reichel's German translations. Selhan Savcigil helped me out, most patiently, when I was baffled by metonymies in poems by Oktay Rifat – not that I know no Turkish, but that poet dovetails references in singular ways. The text from Haroldo de Campos' *Galaxias* was translated in collaboration with Norman Potter: a salute to him now among the shades.

The title of this book is taken from the passage in William Blake's *Vala, or The Four Zoas* (Night the Fifth), where Enitharmon is waiting to give birth to Luvah, King of Love:

But the soft pipe, the flute, the viol, organ, harp, & cymbal,
And the sweet sound of silver voices calm the weary couch
Of Enitharmon . . .
Still the faint harps & silver voices calm the weary couch,
But from the caves of deepest night, ascending in clouds of mist,
The winter spread his wide black wings across from pole to pole.

CHRISTOPHER MIDDLETON

Notes

1. Eric A. Havelock, *The Muse Learns to Write* (New Haven and London: Yale University Press, 1986), p.57.

2. Seamus Heaney, 'Crediting Poetry', originally in *Artes: An International Reader of Literature, Art, and Music* (New York: Mercury House, and Stockholm: Natur och Kultur, 1996), p.18.

3. Alfred Schuler, 'Caena und Thermen, Vortrag 3', in *Fragmente und Vorträge aus dem Nachlaß*, ed. Ludwig Klages (Leipzig 1940), p.194. Schuler's eccentric lecture, delivered in Spring 1915, was heard by Rilke (in Munich): '. . . In the *silentium* the Other World appears . . . through the silence before and after the prayer to the Lares, man recedes and is reabsorbed into . . . the telesmatically glowing world of the ancestors.'

4. *Les vers dorés de Pythagore expliqués / précédés d'un discours sur l'essence et la forme de la poésie.* Paris, 1813. If Rimbaud read Fabre-d'Olivet in Charleville, he might have drawn from this *discours* his own entire project (1870–3) of a visionary poetry 'en avant' (shaping future time).

Introit

OKTAY RIFAT

How the Poem Comes

She comes from the table of foam,
naked, green she brings
from the deep, yellow with mud she comes
dragging dead sea birds to the coffee house
where divers drink, comes
like a cut-throat wind from the south

She comes breaking her maidenhood
with a speed of thought and dizzying, comes
tired, cupping her hands to beggar folk
with the strangled cry of a halfwit.

1. MEMORY

FRIEDRICH HÖLDERLIN

Heidelberg

Long have I loved you and for my own delight
   Would call you mother, give you an artless song,
      You, of all the towns in our country
         The loveliest that ever I saw.

As the forest bird crosses the peaks in flight,
   Over the river shimmering past you floats
      Airy and strong the bridge,
         Humming with sounds of traffic and people.

Once, as if it were sent by gods, enchantment
   Seized me as I was passing over the bridge
      And the distance with its allure
         Shone into the mountainscape,

And that strong youth, the river, was rushing on down
   To the plain, sorrowing-glad, like the heart that overflows
      With beauty and hurls itself,
         To die of love, into the floods of time.

You had fed him with streams, the fugitive, given him
   Cool shadow, and all the shores looked on
      As he followed his way, their image
         Sweetly jockeying over the waves.

But into the valley hung heavy the vast
   And fate-acquainted fort, by lightnings torn
      To the ground it stood on; yet
         Eternal sun still poured

Its freshening light across the giant and aging
   Thing, and all around was green with ivy,
      Living; friendly woodlands ran
         Murmurous down across the fort.

Bushes flowered all down the slope to where,
   In the vale serene, with hills to prop them, shores
   For them to cling to, your small streets
   Mid fragrant garden bowers repose.

c.1800

EDUARD MÖRIKE

The Forsaken Girl

Early, in starlight still,
And the cocks crowing,
I must stand at the hob,
Must get the fire going.

Sparks leap, and lovely
The flames ablaze;
Sunk in sorrow,
At them I gaze.

Suddenly then recall,
Faithless lover,
Last night I dreamed of you,
Over and over.

Tear upon tear now
Tumbling down;
So the day comes and comes –
Would it were gone.

1829

Childhood

Full-berried the elder-bush; tranquilly childhood lived
In a blue cave. Over the bygone path
Where now pale brown the wild grasses hiss,
Calm branches ponder; the rustling of leaves

This too when blue waters sound under the crags.
Gentle the blackbird's plaint. A shepherd
Follows unspeaking the sun that rolls from the autumn hill.

A blue moment is purely and simply soul.
At the forest edge a shy deer shows itself, at peace
Below in the vale the old bells and sombre hamlets rest.

Now more devout, you know the meaning of the dark years,
Coolness and autumn in solitary rooms;
And still in holy azure shining footfalls ring.

An open window softly knocks; tears come
At the sight of the decayed graveyard on the hill,
Memory of told legends; yet the soul sometimes brightens
When she thinks of the glad folk, the dark-gold springtime days.

1913

ABU BAKR IBN 'ABD AL-MALIK IBN QUZMAN

The Crow

That house, not a stone left standing now,
Yet love does bring me back to where it was.

Some whose hour struck are gone for keeps:
Arcade and all, everywhere the wilderness.
The little dove mourns, with its cooing voice.
You love a friend – what's to be hoped for, next?
Simply seek, and mourn, the trace he left.

The soul went out of me. Sooner touch
Starlight than ever, ever it return.
The turtledove, no matter what [. . .]
[. . .]
[. . .]

Ibn Zaid's dive – what was all that noise about?
The busy throng that glittered round the Mosque?
Delight in life! But an evil, greater, beat it down:
Look now, barren field, no plough, no seed.
Desert bigger than a man could grow.

Who'd ever tell it was my haunt, with friends,
Loyal, breezy, after a festival,
Me flashy in fine threads from a cabin trunk,
Hearing the plectrum pick at a guitar,
And shrilling in the open air, a flute.

Quzman repents! Let him get on with it.
Among the other lives, his was a feast.
Now drum is mute, and tambourine, the dance is done.
Still the muezzin inches up his minaret,
And prostrate in a mosque the imam prays.

Sinister twin of his, the crow croaks.
Not a dash of salt about him, poor glum thing!
In mourning garb for ever, never glad:
All in sight or earshot ugliness for him:
Ah, deadly bird, pitchblack, the bogeyman!

Early 12th century

'The Crow' was written after Cordova – ibn Quzman's native city – had been devastated by Berbers egged on by the fundamentalist *faqi*, doctrinaires of Islamic law. This is the penultimate poem in the earliest collection, so-called 'Palestinian', thus presumably one of ibn Quzman's last. Ellipses mark lines lost in the original.

GÜNTER KUNERT

The Polish Tree

There was a tree that stood outside the little town of Kielce but still in sight of it, not a famous tree at all, far from the world, always on the fringe of history.

Out of the foliage which clasps it, the deep green pinnacles, it is said, you can hear on some days a sound of weeping, like children's voices, when the wind blows through the tree, cries and whimpering, sighs which end in rattling sounds, in breathless silence. Not everyone, they say in Kielce, has the right ears to hear what sounds are being made in the trembling branches.

A German scientist, armed with a tape-recorder, lurked for a long time under the huge crown of leaves, without being able to record anything acoustically peculiar; and he assigns to the realm of fable what is said about the tree and the children. He says: apart from the oak-tree and two jays, everything else is scientifically baseless.

1964

GEORG TRAKL

To One Who Died Young

O the black angel who softly stepped from the heart of the tree
When we were gentle playmates in the evening,
By the edge of the pale-blue fountain.
Our step was easy, the round eyes in autumn's brown coolness,
O the purple sweetness of the stars.

But the other descended the stone steps of the Mönchsberg,
A blue smile on his face, and strangely ensheathed
In his quieter childhood, and died;
And the silver face of his friend stayed behind in the garden,
Listening in the leaves or in the ancient stones.

Soul sang of death, the green decay of the flesh,
And it was the murmur of the forest,
The fervid lament of the animals.
Always from dusky towers rang the blue evening bells.

Times came when the other saw shadows in the purple sun,
The shadows of putrescence in the bare branches;
At evening, when by the dusky wall the blackbird sang,
His ghost quietly appeared there in the room.

O the blood that runs from the throat of the musical one,
Blue flower; O the fiery tear
Wept into the night.

Golden cloud and time. In a lonely room
You ask the dead child to visit you more often,
You walk and talk together under elms by the green riverside.

1913

FRIEDRICH HÖLDERLIN

Remembrance

The north-easter is blowing,
Of all winds the one I love
Best, for it promises
Fiery spirit and a good voyage
For seafarers. So go now and greet
The beautiful Garonne
And the gardens of Bordeaux,
Where on the sharp
Riverbank the path
Descends, and deep down
Into the river the brook
Cascades, but
A noble brace of oaks overlooks it,
And silver poplars;

This I do recall and how
With broad crests the elmwood
Arches over the mill,
But in the courtyard grows a fig tree.
There on holidays
Brown women walk
On silken ground,
When March has come
And day and night are equal,
And over slow footpaths,
Weighted with golden dreams,
The lulling breezes move.

But hand me,
Someone, the fragrant cup
Brimming with dark light, that I
May rest; sleep
Would be sweet, in the shadow.
It is not good
To let mortal thoughts
Drain the soul. But conversation
Is good, and to speak

From the heart, to hear tell
Much about days of love
And deeds that have been done.

   Yet where are my friends, Bellarmin
With his companion? Some hesitate
To approach the source;
For it is in the sea
That plenitude begins. They,
Like painters, compose
The beauty that is of earth, and do not shun
Winged war and a life
Years on end alone before the unleafed mast,
Where no town festivals
Make luminous the night,
Nor music, nor native dancing.

   But now to the Indians
The men have gone,
There by the windy point,
By grape-clustering hills, down which
The Dordogne comes, and outward
With the glorious Garonne
Seawide the waters roll. Yet it takes away
Memory, and gives it, the sea does;
Sedulously, too, love steadies the gaze;
What abides, even then, the poets ordain it.

1802–3

Foxholes

It was with eyelashes I gathered my writings up,
tidied their hair,
ant,
oregano,
oakum,
all of a sudden I knew ten people,
sun dropping on the horizon its tremendous lance,
a woman with fat hips loomed from the ferry dock,
all the houses hushed,
look, look at the sea, the well of the sea I lived beside
was watching over us,
on the water, what was it,
a solar eclipse
kept us in the crystal of its silhouette,
from one glass two straws for drinking,
happiness and birds of summer, calm

And added, all unknowing,
way through passionate loves,
the consequences of my feelings,
what did it mean, or better, what was I thinking
ensconced behind a hedge of silence,
breezes hot,
old nags exhausted from dragging their cart,
the glass simply shattered as it stood there,
this uncertain accounting of my life
has to be kept, everyone digs
his own foxhole and falls into it,
because the links from eye to eye will snap,
because our comprehensions fall apart,
the feeling of a person is important,
more so in the salt of yesteryear –

you did not understand me,
lamentable me, talking nonsense, one of you,
name I forget, must take to the road again.

1984

FRIEDERIKE MAYRÖCKER

of burdocks / of the intrepidity of life
(for Jean Améry)

of the wilted
crumpled petals of the wild
willowrose, and rustling
callers to prayer / muezzin – ah! convoking
heart / pressed
moments / skullings / starred
glass – the dried, weatherbeaten
heart / heartleafage / and leafy blooms of
the heart: and how at first light they
are *carted away*, by a grey, freezing, bareheaded
carter, in a barrow, on
a deserted street . . and
swept away . .
like eyeflowers and flowers
of the cheek –
whisperings
behind the door

of burdocks climbing / hurryings
(gone wild) hunters' whistlings,
of rose fleshed
applewood:
his free open heart, this
feeling she'd want to remember it later: how
like braille, without looking,
the pain marked her face
with signs, when
their glances met
(and quietly his head away
across the heads and all among the heads
and as if lost / seeking
head to head / finally:
how was he?
. . and waving waving a last
waving . .
and the wave returned.)

of radiant
places / time-
bell, a bell-tree / of
the moon between mountains, an
aurora – all the world
a fish-hook stage –
and how the deep
shadow – protraction of a
slow leave-taking, by degrees
rescinds itself . .

and that finally
the constant, hard /
pain took hold of her

1982 (written 1978)

OKTAY RIFAT

Going to Üsküdar

Give me the reins
give me the whip
leave me the horses –
Would you like an apple too, he asked
I want no apple, I told the driver,
these are my dead strolling through the tombs.

1984

ROLF DIETER BRINKMANN

Where Are They

Where are they

now? On the yellow writing paper
a few hurried, scribbled

notes, the words like people
who were spilled from the travelling

carnival. We are, both of us,
the curious, the singular

travellers. Now they call to one another
unidentified sounds, happily,

with bright, simple plumage.
So this blue bus drove on and

away. At every stop it left
in waiting rooms a cloud of dust,

which settled slowly, after days,
on upholstered chairs, the tables and

the stone floor. Behind
the steamy windowpanes you see

nobody waiting, none of us. The
stacked automats rust. Their

disguised machinery crumbles like
the empty postcard stands upon

the bar, behind which sleeps
the woman who once, briefly, was

a woman, and stayed behind, her
head propped, a photo, too briefly,

beside the boiling coffee pot. For
five cents anyone can get there,

if there were someone, in the town.
The blue bus, an enormous day,

cloudless, filled with heat, has travelled
on already, and does not repeat

itself. There, into the day, both
of them have gone, enchanted company

of singular persons, both. A
quietness, which

rises out of itself, with doors, to travel
in every direction, and to stop. Both

simply travelled through, and
the past, the pages, both,

is what is simply gone,
to their momentary pleasure

which, changing, endures, slowly,
tenderly, a door: open enough to

remain a secret, empty, which they both
slowly, slowly and precisely, know.

1977

GÜNTER KUNERT

Enigma

There it is, in the clarity
of standing water
where light wallows as if alive.
It wears the colour of night
or fog
rising out of crevices in earth.
Shows the form
of a bare foot
no animal has but you.
It has the sheen of metal
and vanishes like all that draws breath.
The riddle of the world
awaits your solution the moment
you are reminded
to open up your eyes.

1996

FRIEDERIKE MAYRÖCKER

Lost and Near

Don't know why but
suddenly between
Lastenstrasse and the Ring the feeling
came over me again I'd like
once more to see you
Someone
walking toward me looked
like you, I sought
more signs, the white and blue quilt,
the sharp
crusts in ice, a flash
came from a photo automat, the moon
went dimmer, shifted
into the zenith, jackdaws
crisscrossed and called, there was a smell
of baked apples, in my head
something swam, my
eyes were hot, in the illuminated top
angle of the wall your
limbs in a tangle of ivy,
and stretching up and up
your blackened hand . . .

1981

JÜRGEN THEOBALDY

Pearl Harbor Backwards

Pearl Harbor, sweat trickles off me
between lines at the very thought of it,
many American soldiers
in tropical dimestore shirts worn loose
over the belt, the tepid Coke
evaporating in the shade of a palm tree.
On the beach the vamps from inland
were posing, and yesterday night
one boy slit his windpipe with a razor.
Heat wallows through the bars like syrup,
but this morning a gale ripped off
several of these flimsy bamboo roofs.
The cameraman was there at once and filmed
also the Japanese squadrons leaving,
the chattering parrots as they sink
into the foliage, collapsing smoke mushrooms,
Pearl Harbor, that's how I saw it at the movies, twice,
the sweaty smell of an undershirt
filling my nose and eyes, in a back street,
where the projectionist lost control of his projector.
He showed us the pictures in reverse
before the whisky zapped him out.

1976

41

SCOTTISH POETRY LIBRARY
5 Crichton's Close
Edinburgh EH8 8DT
Tel. 0131 557 2876

GÜNTER KUNERT

Travelling Companion

How it happened that
he got lost, no idea.
The trek through time
entails all kinds of losses,
constant quarrelling
about the condition of roads,
and the influence of weather.
Always apportioned anew
(as rations, stuff to chew on) causes
with no nutritional value. Every
'missing' announcement
goes unanswered, because
out of sight out of mind
and it means Oh God.
But then toward nightfall
just now I find
on the snow
bloodflecks
the trace of Your Claws.

1996

ARTHUR RIMBAUD

Memory

I

Lustrous water; salt, of tears a child might shed,
whiteness, of women's bodies that assail the sun;
milk, a multitude, pure lily of the pennon
beneath bastion walls a maid of sorts defended;

angel frolic; – no . . . golden current on the march
swings cool and black and heavy arms of grass. It,
wan, in a bed blue Heaven has canopied,
bespeaks for drape the shade of hill and arch.

II

Ugh! The damp floor distends its limpid broth.
The water puts in tidy beds a pale gold sheen.
Frocks of little girls, an etiolated green,
make willows, birds at pleasure sallying forth.

Plainer than a guinea, eyelid, yellow and warm,
the kingcup – your marital trust, O spouse! –
on the dot of noon, from its dim mirror envies
in hot grey sky the Sphere, its rose and charm.

III

Madame stands too bolt upright in the nearby
field, where sons of toil are snowing; fingers
a parasol; corolla underfoot; she puts on airs;
but look, in flowery verdure children lie

reading their red morocco book. Alas, the man,
like a myriad angels scattering down the road,
makes off beyond the mountain. She, all cold,
all black, is running after him – he's gone.

IV

Regret, no more the thick young arms of pure grass.
Gold of April moons in the heart of holy bed!
Joy, derelict shanties by the river, August nights haunted
and made it sprout, this putrid carcass!

Now beneath the ramparts, let her weep. Downfloat
of breath from poplars, her one and only breeze.
Then the puddle, grey, no source, no images;
an ancient dredger drudges in his idle boat.

V

Toy of this bleak water eyeball, I can find,
o skiff becalmed, o arms that are too short,
no flower to pick, not the yellow one, importunate,
there, nor the blue, the ashen water's friend.

Ah! powder from willow trees a wingbeat shook!
Roses of rushes, eaten an age ago.
My skiff aground for ever; chain dragged deep below
this water's boundless eye, down to what muck?

1872–3 (?)

JOHANN WOLFGANG VON GOETHE

Euphrosyne

Even the crests of the highest mountain, jagged and icy,
    Gloaming and purple quit, now with the sun going down.
Darkness cloaked the ravine long ago, the wanderer's climbing
    Path by the torrent, he longs soon to arrive at the hut,
Goal of his day, the quiet abode of a mountain shepherd,
    And there is heavenly sleep hurries enticing ahead,
Sleep that sweetly befriends any traveller; may it with sacred
    Poppy garland my head, blessing me also today.
But now what is this gleam from the cliff over yonder, a radiance
    Filling with delicate light vapours that lift from the foam?
Is it the sun, through secret clefts and crevices haply
    Shining? This ambient sheen scarcely belongs to the earth.
Closer it floats, the cloud, it is glowing, I gaze at the marvel;
    Rosy the light, is its ray shaped like a figure that moves?
What goddess is this who comes to me? Which of the Muses
    Might in the chasm so grim search for a trustable friend?
Beautiful goddess, make yourself known to me, do not by vanishing
    Baffle the mind you inspire, thwart all the feelings you touch.
Speak, if you may, your sacred name to a mortal being;
    If that is not to be done, rouse up my passion to feel
Which you may happen to be of Zeus's eternal daughters,
    Then may the poet in song utter your praises at once.
'Do you not know any more, good friend, who I am? This visible
    Form you adored, can it be strange to you now and so soon?
True, I belong to the earth no more, my shuddering spirit,
    Sorrowful, flew from the world's pleasure and gladness and youth;
Yet did I hope that the mind of my friend would carry my image
    Firmly imprinted, and more, make it transfigured by love.
Yes, now I see and feel from your gaze, from your tears I can tell it:
    Well he knows who she is: Euphrosyne I am.
Look you, she who has gone before must walk in the mountain
    Forest, seeking him out, faraway travelling man,
Seeking her teacher, friend, her father, again she is looking
    Back to the joys of the earth, in their provisional frame.
Let me remember when I was a child and the art of dissembling,
    Games of the ravishing Muse, these you tutored me in.
Every moment and tinier detail let me remember;

Ah, what a pleasure we take; putting a mind to what's lost!
Sweetness of days on earth, the airiest, all in a torrent,
    Ah, who can prize them enough, treasures that trickle away?
Small it may seem to us now, but ah, to the heart never petty;
    Love, to be sure, and art, magnify things that are small.
Do you recall the time when, there on the stage, you taught me
    Serious matters indeed, higher demands of the art?
I appeared as a boy, very winsome, and "Arthur" you called me –
    You were restoring, in me, life to an Englishman's play,
Threatened my eyes with fire you did, with fire, it was terrible,
    Turning away as you wept, under the spell of the scene.
Ah! and then you were kind, protecting a life full of sorrow
    Which precipitate flight finally stole from the boy.
Me, shattered, you took in your friendly arms and away and
    Then for a little I feigned death as I lay on your breast.
Finally, though, I opened my eyes and saw you, so serious,
    Rapt in thought as you gazed down at your darling-in-arms.
Childishly up I reached and kissed your hands, being thankful,
    Offered my charming mouth, chaste was the kiss we exchanged,
Then I asked you: Why so serious? If I'm a failure,
    Tell me, father, I pray, how to do better next time.
Nothing I'll grudge you, gladly rehearse for you, over and over,
    Each and every part, follow your lessons and leads.
But you held me firm in your arms and hugged me more tightly,
    And in my bosom I felt trembling the throb of my heart.
No, my charmingest child, you answered me, people tomorrow –
    Show to them all you have shown, just as you showed it today.
Move them all, as me you have moved, and they will respond with
    Even the driest of eyes weeping their tears of applause.
None will be struck more deeply, yet, than the friend, whom corpses
    Horrified once in the past, holding you now in his arms.
Nature, ah, how certain and grand in all things appearing:
    Heaven and Earth must obey firm and immutable laws.
One year follows another, the summer extending to springtime,
    Winter to fullness of fall, a confident helping hand.
Masses of rock stand their ground, and the waters eternal
    Gush from the cloudy cleft, foaming and thundering down.
Firs are green and unleafed bushes, even in winter,
    Tend clandestine buds, ready to sprout from their twigs.
Everything comes to be and perishes lawfully, only
    Human delectable life suffers a wavering fate.
Not to the son who is reaching the flower of youth does a father

Nod from the brink of the grave, willing to die as he must.
It is not always the young who shut the eyes of the old folk,
    Eyes that are willing to close, frailty yielding to strength.
Fate will reverse, more often, the sequence of days, and a person
    Full of his years must lament children and grandchildren dead,
Stand like a stricken bole, the broken branches around him
    Scattered on every side, ripped by the torrents of hail.
Such were the thoughts, my beautiful child, that bore down upon me,
    When as a corpse you hung feigning a death in my arms.
But what a joy to see you again, in the glow of your girlhood,
    Creature I love very much, close to my heart and revived.
Off with you now, and be glad, little boy in disguise! For the girl will
    Grow to enrapture the world, captivating me quite!
Strive as you strove today; and, as for your natural talent,
    Climbing the ladder of life may it be modelled by art.
Be my delight for years to come, may your beautiful gift be
    Perfect before my eyes finally close on the world –
Those were your words, an important moment, I'll never forget it,
    Later I grew to be me, thanks to your speech so sublime.
O how I loved to address to people the stirring orations,
    Weighty with meaning, your words, placed on the lips of a child.
When you were watching, O how I grew, I was seeking you always
    Out in the public below, people entirely amazed.
Yet that is where you will be, you will stand there, and Euphrosyne,
    Never again will she step forward to brighten your glance.
You will not hear them again, the sounds of the voice of your pupil,
    Which you so early attuned, early, to passionate grief.
Others come and they go; for others will certainly please you.
    Even a talent that's great fades when a greater one comes.
But don't ever forget me. If anyone ever comes brightly   ·
    Forward to meet you amid vague goings-on of the day,
Follows the signals you give and basks in the smile of your favour,
    Never desiring a place other than that you appoint,
Sparing herself not at all, but working, actively, gladly
    Sacrificing her all, up to the gate of the grave –
Friend, be mindful of me, I ask you, say, sooner or later,
    Euphrosyne again! Back to me she has come!
Much besides I would like to say; but a spirit departing
    Cannot stop as she will; strictly I'm led by a god.
Fare thee well! I am hurried away by a vague commotion.
    Listen, I have one wish: kindly grant it, my friend:
Let me not go down unmagnified into the shadows!

Only the Muse can endow death with an inkling of life.
For there are floating, in the domain of Persephoneia,
  Multitudes without shape, shadows bereft of all name;
Whomsoever the poet will praise, though, walks with a difference,
  Has an identity, formed, joins in the heroes' choir.
Joy will be winging my step, if a song from you has announced me,
  Gracious upon me will rest, also, the goddess's gaze.
Then she'll receive me with clemency, speaking my name, and the others,
  Goddesses, close to the throne, lofty women, will wave.
That most loyal of women, Penelope, she will address me,
  Also Euadne, who clings close to the husband she loves.
Later the others will come who were sent below prematurely,
  Near me there will be girls, grieving with me for our fate.
When Antigone comes, of all the souls most like a sister,
  Also Polyxena, still dark with her death as a bride,
I shall be seeing them all as sisters, joining their number,
  For of the tragical art delicate creatures they are.
Me, too, shaped I was by a poet, and some of his poems,
  Yes, for me, will complete moments denied me in life.' –
Thus did she speak and still with her sweet lips open and moving,
  Making as if to speak, only a whirring I heard.
For from the purple cloud as it floated, always in motion,
  Imperturbable strode Hermes the glorious god.
Gently he lifted his staff and pointed: billowing vapours
  Waxed more dense, and the two – swallowed up into them, gone.
Night more darkly presses around me, tumultuous waters
  Thunder now more loud, flanking the slippery path.
Stricken I am, with a sorrow unbearable, shocked with the pity,
  Weak, I lean on a rock, feeling the moss with a hand.
Misery sweeps the strings of my heart, a dark weeping
  Flows; and over the trees comes a first shimmer of dawn.

1798

'Euphrosyne' (Οἰφροσύνη) in Greek means 'gaiety'. The poem is an elegy for the young actress Christiane Neumann, news of whose death at the age of nineteen reached Goethe while he was travelling in Switzerland in 1797. He had rehearsed her for a production of Shakespeare's *King John* in the Weimar theatre. The elegy is remarkably self-reflexive: the shade in the poem asks that a poem should be written to legitimize her kinship with Greek shade-heroines in the Underworld, and, being written in classical elegiac couplets, the poem would certainly legitimize itself in the hearing of those Greeks.

2. LOVES

RAINER MARIA RILKE

Sonnets to Orpheus II, 4

This is the beast that happens not to be.
They did not know yet loved it with a will,
Its walk, its neck, the way that it stood still,
The light in its calm eyes they loved to see.

True, it was not. But as they loved it so,
Pure beast, it came to be. They even gave
A space to it, vacant and clear, and though
There it lifted up its head, it did not have

To be. They did not nourish it with corn
But always with the possibility it might
Just be. This made in it such vigour stir

It put a horn forth from its brow. One horn.
Toward a virgin girl it came, all white,
And was, in her silver mirror, and in her.

1922

The Quince

Yellow its colour
As if it wore
A daffodil slip
A perfume
Penetrating as musk

Perfumed and hard of heart
As that woman I want
Mine its colour, lover-colour
Passionate, strong

It is pale with a pallor
Loaned from the midst of me
And when she breathes
She breathes its deep odour

It had grown on a branch
Ripe in its odour
And leaves by then had woven
Brocade for its mantle

Hand outstretched
Gently I picked it
In the middle of my room
I placed it with reverence
A censer

Rolled
In ashes, fuzz
Its golden body

Naked in my hand
Under its daffodil slip

It made me think of her
I cannot name
I was breathing so hard
My fingers crushed it

Before 982

FRIEDRICH HÖLDERLIN

The Farewell
Second version

Did we intend to part, thinking it good and wise?
  Why did the act once done shock us like murder? Ah,
    Little we understand
      Ourselves, for a god is in us.

Fail him? Ah, fail the one who for us created
  All meaning and all life, into our love
    Put life and soul, guarding it,
      This one thing I cannot do.

But meaning a different fault the world's intent
  Practises a different task, hard, different laws;
    Custom and habit snaffle
      Day by day the soul from us.

So be it. I knew as much. Since ever rooted
  Malformity, fear, cleft gods and men apart,
    Must with blood to atone them
      Mortal hearts in love pass on.

Do not have me speak, let me never again behold
  This deadly thing, that I may make my way in peace,
    At least, into solitude,
      And let this parting be our own.

Hand me the cup yourself, that I with you may drink
  The holy bane, enough, the saving draft, and drink
    Lethe's oblivion, that we may both
      Forget the hate and the love also.

I go, willing. Long hence, perhaps, Diotima, I
  Shall see you here. But wishes will have bled away,
    And all at peace, like souls
      Of the departed, we shall walk about,

Strangers, conversation leading us up and down,
   Pensive, hesitant, though now the place of our farewell
    Reminds us, who shall be forgotten,
      A heart grows warm in us,

I look at you with wonder, voices I hear and sweet
   Song as from a time gone by, and music of strings,
    And the lily wafts to us,
      Golden, its fragrance above the stream.

1800 (?)

A Dirge of the Wise Man of Paris

To love – just these ephemeral skirts alone?
It'd be like saying 'Happy Centenary' to the sun.

But in their fugitive gardens you can taste, unique,
A concourse of the All at their dolls' picnic;

Taste, conducting rites that are reciprocal,
Unconscious stuff, boiled, in their eggshell.

Executor, perhaps, of the Law's writ and Estate,
With all your faith you will pontificate;

These anonymous solfeggios, perhaps, you'll vivisect
For the art of it, and never their ultimate *do* expect,

For don't think that the host where sleeps your heaven
Has in its flour an unimagined leaven.

Well, anyway, their eyes are all! And the table's laid,
On the juvenile Organ blind improvisations are played,

And – no wedding, honeymoon, or baggage at all,
No cancans, no shared bed stale as the air in a hospital –

But a stately stained glass window in your home,
And living together solo, is still not so dumb.

See her then, and loyally, as otherwise
The people walking past, the words, the things, the skies.

Pluck your grapes from the childish arts; be gay,
With a fugue, a word, a tune, an air of holiday.

Science – what knowledge can it ever bequeathe? –
Finds, like balloons, the Dark where none can breathe.

Never force your talent for being a creature;
All is decreed, all true, nothing contra nature.

To live weighing all by the Good, the Beautiful, the True?
O perfumes, o looks, o faiths, o well, I'll give it a go;

But like Brennus with his sword and in advance
Aren't I, too, weighed in the balance?

The True, the Beautiful, the Good – trays marked 'out' and 'in';
Be in accord, be large: the Law will know its kin.

Ah, your swaddlings of the Occident might see some changes,
Child, if you drink your fill from the Ganges!

Logic, morality – so much talk;
But – layers of instinct, where paradises lurk,

Night of heredity, limbos of latencies –
Active, passive? O lawns of faintnesses,

Sieve of pores! Depths under the ocean's welter,
Absolute virgin forest, Infinite without shelter!

To see, heave the plummet out, or dive below the bell,
O like eels under rock velleities coil,

Sneaky polyps attending the hook,
Unregistered vows, wishes that suit no book,

Geysers of guano, stars in a swooning slide,
Metals that make our spectroscopes cross eyed!

A pod bursts, giving a world of matters
The itch, to populate the heights it scatters,

Others lurch beneath genetical tackling,
Or set in their labs a hellfire crackling.

Well then, let it go, let it be, and Love
Will know his own: being both blind and deaf.

For countless life goes out, fanning the seeds toward
Concurrent beings with no rights or ultimate reward.

Rub along, go ahead, the All-Potent blesses you:
There is your pity, your love, and your *bon goût*.

The Unconscious – with that Eastern Eden all things brim;
Earth won't dry up if that's where she can swim.

It is the Great Nanny, our loves she gave us,
By divine selection's magnanimous favours.

It is the True Tree, the omniversal ombellar man-
Chineel we sleep, babes, under, while we can.

('Scientific discoveries' we choose to call
The dead leaves that seasonally from it fall.)

There, on cushions of ethical etiquette,
With regular lyric purrs levitate, like a cat,

Not dreaming: 'Am I me? So complicated, this!
Where might I be now? What boat did I miss?'

With a wan faith, don't rage or laugh or agonize,
At opulent flirtings of quibblous displays

(Never pretending, for that is indecorous)
Sip every day your cup of nothingness;

Washed like a wafer, in white or black motley costumes,
Flutter, brief calyx which any least nuance perfumes.

'– But everything mocks Justice! and whence comes my heart,
My sacred heart, ah, if it rhymes with nought?'

Rest up, with flowers. Can it be your concern,
What you were, in the Forever, before you were born?

Well then, the other eternity still, void of your presence,
Will swarm – may it leave you cold, but with due reverence.

As for *your* death, its blind flash is on the way,
And it will *thingummy* you, whatever you say.

'It's laughing with birds, the pine they'll carpenter
For my coffin, but *yours* will be *its* death,' etcetera . . .

Perfect, you take my point. Bend your whole mind, no less,
To living without intent now, mad with gentleness.

1885 (Written 1884)

To Anna Flower

O thou beloved of my twenty seven senses,
I love thine! – Thou thine thee thou,
I to thee, thou to I. – We?
That (incidentally) is beside the point.
Who art thou, countless female? Thou art – art
thou? – People say thou'd be – let them talk,
they don't know chalk from cheese.
Hat on foot thou walkst upon
thy hands, upon thou hands thee walk.
Hi there! Red clothes of thine, sawn into
white folds. Red I love Anna Flower, red
I love thine! Thou thine thee thou,
I to thee, thou to I. – We?
That (incidentally) belongs in the ashbox.
Red Flower, red Anna Flower, what do people say?
Prize question: 1. Anna Flower is a weird bird.
                  2. Anna Flower is red.
                  3. What colour is the bird?
Blue is the colour of thy yellow hair.
Red is the cooing of thy green bird.
Thou neat maid in an ordinary dress, thou
sweet green animal, I love thine!
Thou thine thee thou, I to thee, thou to I. – We?
That (incidentally) belongs in the emberchest.
Anna Flower! Anna, a-n-n-a, I drip thy name.
Thy name drips like soft beef suet.
Dost realize, Anna, dost realize it?
People can read thee back to front and thee, thee
most glorious girl, art both ways round: a-n-n-a.
Beef suet dripplestroke across my back.
Anna Flower, thou drippy animal, I love thine!

1919

ABU BAKR IBN 'ABD AL-MALIK IBN QUZMAN

Zakhal to Umm al-Hakam

How could I not be sad, living apart
From her, if Umm al-Hakam kept my heart?

Faithful to her, it never quits her side.
Each day I'm gone is longer than a month.
I've lost my occupation, lost my moon.
The moment I forsook her, sorrows came.

A seething lonesomeness deep down inside.
Queen of the world, to her I should return.
Years and months pass by and they are gone.
My love for Umm al-Hakam does not pass.

Among her neighbours, rightly she may boast:
Her skin the tint of pomegranate flowers,
Her eyes so large, their concentrated dark
Spellbinds anyone, or leaves its scars.

Her kiss, O what a sweetness in its taste.
That little mouth, subtle and fine her lips:
Forget, I tell myself, no pact they sealed:
Remember times we lived as one, at peace.

Be true and constant (as your lover is).
Stay home; and please, if you go out, go veiled.
Anyone who speaks well of me, believe.
Don't credit any gossip from the crones.

My messenger will come, receive him well.
If you can stoop to write a letter, then
I will break off a bone to be my pen,
And write with it, in blood, a fit reply.

Early 12th century

My tiny one, if your eyes are tired from gazing,
If you let me call you brotherkin,
Me, blue-eyed, I ask of you
Lift very high the flower of your life.
I'm like you. I dropped from a cloud, hurt
Was done me, because, different, unfit
For society, I was nowhere loved.
What do you say? We'll be like brother
And sister. Think: we are
People, free, on free earth. Us, we
Make the rules no-one should fear, not ever,
And in the clay we model action. I know
You are lovable, pale blue flower,
And I am so spry and so sudden
When you speak of Sotchi,
And open wide your gentle eyes.
I who have so long doubted, doubted many things,
Suddenly and forever I believe. It is written,
Down there, that the woodchopper whacks
With his axe in vain. We'll elude
Many futile sayings,
Simply I'll serve you mass in the morning,
Like the priest maned with long tresses; drink
From blue streams the purity. And fearsome names,
They will not frighten us.

1921

Dated 13 September 1921; translated from the French version
by Luda Schnitzer – Velimir Khlebnikov, *Choix de poèmes*,
Paris 1967, p.205. Original first published in 1923. Probably
the flower *myosotis* – forget-me-not – is being addressed.

JOHANN WOLFGANG VON GOETHE

Autumn Feeling

More fatly greening climb
The trellis, you, vine leaf
Up to my window!
Gush, denser, berries
Twin, and ripen
Shining fuller, faster!
Last gaze of sun
Broods you, maternal;
Of tender sky the fruiting
Fullness wafts around you;
Cooled you are, by the moon
Magic, a friendly breath,
And from these eyes,
Of ever quickening Love, ah,
Upon you falls a dew, the tumid
Brimming tears.

1775

ALBERT GLATIGNY

Idiot Girl

1

Baby with a walk so slow,
So nonchalant and so serene,
I love the squabby way you go,
I love you, idiot beauty queen!

A mirror of your oafishness,
Or in a hearth cold coals that see
No poker come to make a blaze,
Your gentle eyes, they ravish me.

Forehead squat, crushed underneath
Thick red hair – but upward bent
Your nose rapels, when you draw breath,
A peak of pure astonishment.

The way your massive bosom quakes,
I must admit, somewhat alarms me,
Yet an imbecilic grace
Inherent in the wobble charms me.

Me you enchant, intoxicate:
Beside you, taunting promises
I think I hear, that you will let
The good times roll, in carnal bliss.

When I taste, upon your lips,
The crusted honey of your kisses,
When your huge arm my body clips
And almost breaks my bones in pieces,

Then I'm happy. Even if
That girl I fancied once, the nymphet,
Came by again, confessed her love,
I'd answer her: Back off now, limpet!

There's not a woman known to men,
In heaven not a single goddess,
Intoxicates me quite as when
Your liquid gaze is on me, honest.

Very strange, that squiffy state,
Ah! If I could for once abstain!
The wines you mix intoxicate,
Addle the sense and stun the brain.

Creature robust, my heart's elect,
Because I droop, you thrill me through.
Tortured by my intellect
I like the nuttiness of you!

2

So lay you down, great love machine,
Proud in body and triumphant
Submit yourself, to fate resign
Like a tractable young elephant.

All the hate that fills my heart
Conspires with love on seeing *thee*,
A speechless mass, opaque, prostrate
In blazing sunshine, there for me.

I feel: this animal, wild and savage,
I have teased it; yet I think:
Likely it will pounce and ravage
If I look away or wink.

That is why, my gentle friend,
My eyes on yours are firmly fixed,
And why, now hardened in my hand,
I wield aloft this solid stick.

Yet, like a panther trapped, you fling
A look at me, bewildered, and –
Now my finger is your bung –
Dejected ask me: What you want???

With your mouth my mouth refresh,
For this mouth of mine is thirsty;
I relish smells of primal flesh
From your body's volumes bursting.

Your force combined with something soft
Concocts a sort of seasoning
That's brisk, bizarre, and it has left
The taste of chili on my tongue.

Your solid shoulders in the light
Suffice entirely, yet, to prove
Credulous aspiration trite,
Absurd the reveries of love.

Come the day, noble palliasse,
Quivering beast, but girl created
Sacred Matter's masterpiece,
When I'm in you annihilated!

1864

The source of the original is *Oeuvres complètes* (Paris: Alphonse Lemerre, nd).
Glatigny (1839–73) came from a poor Norman family, discovered at an early
age in the family attic an edition of Ronsard, and lived thereafter a Bohemian
life dedicated to poetry. Sporadically he was celebrated in Paris by Banville,
Mendès, Coppée and other slightly younger poets, including Verlaine
(Rimbaud would have known his work). Mallarmé, whom he visited for a
month in Tournon (1864) wrote an article on him (which disappeared), and in
a letter of June 27, 1864, wrote to Armand Renaud: 'It's marvellous what beau-
tiful things there are in this book (*Les flèches d'or*), written at the whim of inspi-
ration.' Glatigny often attached himself to travelling theatre companies, but he
was given only walk-on parts. For a time in 1867 he earned a fair living in the
Montmartre café 'Alcazar' improvising (between vaudeville songs and the
trapeze act) poems rhymed to suit the customers' pleasure. His first book
appeared in 1860, *Les vignes folles*; 'L'Idiote' appeared in *Les flèches d'or*
(1864). Political verse satires he wrote during the Franco-Prussian war and the
Commune appeared after his death. Shortly before he died of TB, he married
a girl called Emma Dennie (of American origin, but raised in France), who also
died of TB a few months later (a curious foreshadowing of Laforgue and Leah
Lee in 1887 and 1888). Much of Glatigny's work is dated, but 'L'Idiote' has a
freshness and wickedness unusual enough to be worth saving – and so does the
report that it was he who converted Verlaine, in 1867, from beer to the demon
absinthe.

AT-TURTUSHI

Absence

I search the sky
What if by chance
I find up there
A star you see

Travellers pass
What if I ask
If one of them
Inhaled your fragrance

Wind on my face
I feel what if
By chance it might
Bring news of you

On roads I drift
Hearing song on song
What if by chance
One breathed your name

Face after face I meet
Only to look away
What if in one I see
Your beauty's trace

1100 (?)

Four Poems to Ibn Zaydun

Wait for me whenever darkness falls,
For night I see contains a secret best.
If the heavens felt this love I feel for you,
The sun would not shine, nor the moon rise,
Nor would the stars launch out upon their journey.

*

Must separation mean we have no way to meet?
Ay! Lovers all moan about their troubles.
For me it is a winter not a trysting time,
Crouching over the hot coals of desire.
If we're apart, nothing can be otherwise.
How soon just the very thing I feared
Was what my destiny delivered. Night after night
And separation going on and on and on,
Nor does my being patient free me from
The shackles of my longing. Please God
There may be winter rains pelting copiously down
To irrigate the earth where you now dwell.

*

Had you any respect for the love between us,
You would not choose that slave of mine to love.
From a branch flowering in beauty you turn
To a branch that bears no fruit.
You know I am the moon at full,
But worse luck for me
It's Jupiter you have fallen for.

*

They'll call you the Hexagon, an epithet
Properly yours even after you drop dead:
Pederast, pimp, adulterer,
Gigolo, cuckold, cheat.

1050 (?)

JOHANN WOLFGANG VON GOETHE

Amor as Landscape Painter

Sat upon a rocky peak at daybreak,
Staring fix-eyed through the mist before me;
Stretched like canvas primed with grey it mantled
Everything on either side and upward.

A little boy now came and stood beside me:
Friend, he said, I wonder what you're up to,
Peering, supine, at that empty canvas.
Might you have lost for now, if not for ever,
Pleasure in painting, shaping out an image?

Glancing at the child, I thought in secret:
Perhaps the boy thinks he can act the master.

If you sit there, sullen, doing nothing,
Said the boy, no good will be the outcome.
Watch, I'll paint a smidgeon of a picture
Now, for you, a pretty one to learn from.

Then he lifted up his index finger,
Which was quite as rosy as a rose is;
Pointing to the fabric stretched before him,
Now the boy began to trace a picture.

At the top a beauteous sun he painted,
I was almost blinded by the dazzle;
Borders of the clouds, he made them golden,
Rays of sun to perforate the cloud mass;
Painted then the delicate and tender
Tops of freshly quickened trees, with hillocks
Touched into place and freely grouped behind them;
Lower down – water he put, and plenty,
Drew the river, as it is in nature,
So much so, it seemed to glint with sunlight
And murmur as it rose against its edges.

Ah, beside the river flowers had sprouted,
And the meadow was a blaze of colour,

Gold, enamel sheen, a green, and crimson,
All aglow like emerald and carbuncle.
Bright and clear, above, he glazed the sky in,
Mountains, blue, receding in the distance,
So that born anew I looked, ecstatic,
Now upon the painter, now the picture.

You'll admit, says he, I've demonstrated
This is a handiwork I have some skill in;
The hardest part is still to come, however.

Then, with pointing fingertip and very
Solicitously, by the little forest,
Right on the brink of it, where sunlight gathered
To be reflected off the shining humus,
He traced the loveliest girl you could set eyes on,
Pretty figure, and a graceful garment,
Cheeks a fresh complexion, all around them
Tawny hair, and more, the cheeks were tinted
Like the tiny finger that had shaped them.

Little boy, I now exclaimed, what master
Can it be who took you as his pupil,
That your designs should be so swift, so clever,
And finished, as by nature, to perfection?

Even as I'm speaking, look, a zephyr
Gently stirs, it agitates the treetops,
Ruffles all the river into wavelets,
Fills the filmy robe that she is wearing,
The perfect girl, amazed I am, and more so
When she starts to set her feet in motion,
And she moves, she walks, she's coming this way
To where I sit beside my wicked teacher.

Now everything, but everything was moving,
Trees, the flowers, filmy robe, the river,
Delicate feet of the girl in all her beauty –
Do you think I sat so calm and steadfast
Rocklike on my rock a moment longer?

1787

71

IBN KHARUF

The Young Tailor

Sons of Mugara, in your tribe,
Under cover of your lances,
A little antelope, mine, can play
Among the hawthorns hide and seek.

The stool he perches on might be a horse,
A horse, proud of the hero riding it,
A hero, armed with nothing but a needle,
A needle like an eyelash, one of his.

When he puts the stitches in a cloak of silk
His needle, like a shooting star,
Leaves a trail of light,
His thread, behind it.

When he stops
Embroidering a cloak with stripes, every tongue
Wants to be the cushion into which
His needle sticks.

His little thread, him twisting it,
Twists my heart. Please God
My heart may go
Along with him as his thread does.

1200 (?)

QASMUNA BINT ISMA'IL AL-YAHUDI

Seeing Herself Beautiful and Nubile

I see an orchard
Where the time has come
For harvesting,
But I do not see
A gardener reaching out a hand
Toward its fruits.
Youth goes, vanishing; I wait alone
For somebody I do not wish to name.

12th century

OKTAY RIFAT

Coming

I'll come when I'm dead,
jumping the stone,
back at your window,
shine in your candle,
the shadowy road,
I'll wait there for silence,
not staying I'll come
for the daylight with rain,
I'll come, just you wait,
come when the hour strikes,
somebody going,
gone with the nightfall.

1984

3. ART AND ARTIFICE

EDUARD MÖRIKE

On a Lamp

Not yet disturbed, O lovely lamp, you still adorn,
Gracefully suspended here on slender chains,
The ceiling of this pleasaunce, near-forgotten now.
On your white marble bowl, around whose rim is twined
A wreath of ivy leaves in greenish golden bronze,
Children happily join to dance a roundelay.
What charm throughout! laughing, yet the whole form
Ringed by a gentle flowing spirit of seriousness.
A work of art, the genuine thing. Who notices it?
Yet blithely beauty seems to shine in self-content.

1846

Archaic Torso of Apollo

We did not know his unexampled head
in which the eyeballs ripened. None the less
his torso still is glowing like a lantern
and on a lowered flame his gaze inside it

persists and gleams. Or else the bow curve
of the breast could not dazzle you, and in the loins'
gradual turn a smile could never travel
to that midpoint that carried procreation.

Or else this stone would stand deformed and short
beneath the shoulders' glassy cataract,
and would not flicker so, like animal skins;

and would not break from all its confines outward,
rayed like a star: for there's no part of it
that does not see you. You must change your life.

1908

ABU'L HASAN 'ALI IBN HISN

The Dove

The surprise of my life:
On a bough between
Isle and river a dove

Cooing, his collar
Pistache green, lapis his breast,
Neck shimmering and maroon

His back and wingtips.
Pupils of ruby, over them eyelids
Of pearl flitted, trimmed with gold,

Black the point
Of his beak, like
The tip of a reed

Dipped in ink. On the arak bough,
His throne, throat now hid
In the fold of a wing, he rested.

But he saw me weep.
Scared by a sob
On the bough he stood,

Spread wings, beat them,
Took as he flew my heart
Away. Where? I know not.

11th century

LARS GUSTAFSSON

Elegy on the Density of the World

While Nicola Pisano is carving in Pisa
reliefs out of the Baptistery marble,

evidently he knows there is a problem.
Behind every image another is lurking.

Even at sea it is so.
In Nicola's images, pushing and shoving,

Apostles, Soldiers, Horses, Wise Men,
one horse peering across another's withers.

Just so this image fills to the brim.
No help: there's always more to follow,

Apostles, Soldiers, Horses, Wise Men, more soon
surge forward, jostling one another,

there isn't marble enough in Carrara for all of it!
Children are spellbound by sieves and colanders,

drag them out of the kitchen closet, hold them up,
reverently, to the world. And see, as they do so,

Sieve and Behind-Sieve at the same time.
How dense it is, the world they drifted into!

The depth of this intensity horrifies us,
and isn't it strictly prohibited to dream

of standing face to face with a final image?

Or perhaps we dream of a breathing space:
being enfolded a moment in a single image,

exhaling in it. And being one with it:
image in image, briefly, still in stillness.

Till the storm breaks loose again with full force.

1990

80

JOHANN WOLFGANG VON GOETHE

Landscape

So blithe, the whole depicted scene,
The farmer's house, washed bright and clean,
Grass and tree as in morning dew,
The hem of hills a splendid blue.
Look now, the little cloud up there
At play and cooling in pure air!
A Netherlander, if he came
And set up house inside the frame,
Would see and paint what could be sold
As if it were a century old.

How does it all look to you?
Transparent, as if shining through
A skein of silver, or lamplight
Behind the picture charms the sight:
Whatever was ugly and vague before
Such delicate light makes ultra-pure,
A limpid ray illumining
Any quotidian humdrum thing.
If you lack the mind or entrance fee
For art, love lets you in for free.

c. 1813

PETER HUCHEL

Wei Dun and the Old Masters

Marvelling at the old masters,
Who painted boulders as bones of the earth
And thin mists as the skin of hills,
I had tried, with vertical brush,
With quick strokes and slow ones,
To colour the moist radiance of rain.

But as moon and sun shone
On land going more and more to ruin
It was not boulders that were the earth's bones –
Human bones were grinding in the sand
Where tanks ripped with guzzling tracks
Roads open to their grey marrow.

Old masters, I scraped the paint block,
I cleaned the brush of goat hair.
Yet as I rambled behind the foe
I saw the meadows waterless,
The mill wheel shattered, in hardened gear
The ox hang rigid in the whim shaft,
The temple porch plundered
Where on glazed tiles in a heap
The snake dozed all the white noon.

Old masters, how can I paint
The river's rocky dorsal fins
As if, in the shallows, there was lurking
Some giant fish with gills of sun.
And paint the cool bloom of the mist,
The grey whiteness of buoyant snowy air,
As if soft feathers floated from a windy nest.

Where, where have they gone, your heavens,
Into what distances, exalted masters,
The breath of the world, so vulnerable?
Images of terror visited me
And etched my eye with smoke and sorrow.

Where have you gone, Boatman Playing the Flute?
Do you watch in the rain the wild geese flying?
Over the river at night a moaning went.
Your wife with a smoking branch raked
Ashes and embers of your bamboo hut,
To discover there your blackened skull.

And Old Man Going Home from a Village Feast,
Quietly riding your water buffalo,
Through the coolness of falling dew,
Didn't your servant stop in horror
And let the rope loosely hang down?
You rode the buffalo behind the cliff.
By then the foe was at your door.

Where is the Farm by the Lake, fanned
By a chevelure of trees and grasses?
And where in the snow, filtered through mist,
The lonely Village in the High Mountains?
Search behind the penfold of the fire.
War has baked all things dry
In this kiln of death.

Where are the voices, noises of gongs,
The odour of pigment, you poets and painters
Of the Landscape Populated by Scholars?
Dumb, on the level field, how you lie,
Robbed of your shoes, your amulets,
Abandoned to the birds and winds.

Heaven and Earth sustain
Still the ten thousand things.
Deep down, the bones rot.
But the breath flies upward,
Flowing as light you walked through once,
Old masters, with great composure.

1963

GÜNTER KUNERT

From the Background of a Breughel

This ancient house
in the pictures of distance,
forever surrounding:

so the heavens talk to it,
trees and bushes
long ago came and keep
company with it –
the wild grape vine
belts and circles
rooms of sleep,
dark tripes of staircase
the kitchen midpoint
lit by a log and eyes
of cats

Not even crows
ruffle your flesh,
here it is, no longer
waiting, it is your blood
feeds the beams and the tiles,
the rain has wet your skin
for centuries, or only
as long as you are looking

1980

OKTAY RIFAT

For a Picture of the Sea

Sunlit brilliant water,
echo of the Fire,
slippery as a fish,
tensile sideways across the sand,
and leaning on its elbow,
pregnant, scattering light, as,
in that old picture,
the Dutch merchant's wife.

1984

KURT SCHWITTERS

To a Drawing by Marc Chagall: Poem 28

Card harps fish, head in the window.
Animal head lusts the bottle.
On leap-mouth.
Headless man.
Hand wags acid knives.
Card fish lavish dumpling bottle.
And a tabledrawer.
Idiotic.
And button globes inky tablewise.
Fish presses table, stomach sickens sword swish.
A drunkard's stalk eyes inane the lamentanimal,
Eyes parch for the bottle's odour, very.

c. 1920

JOHANN WOLFGANG VON GOETHE

Explanation of an Old Woodcut Depicting Hans Sachs' Poetic Mission

Sunday morning in his shop,
Here's our good master standing up:
He's doffed his dirty apron skin,
A festive doublet now he's in,
Gives hammer and thread and knife a rest,
His awl put back in his workchest;
Now takes he seventh day repose
From cutting up and hammer blows.

Now warms the springtime sun his mind,
Rest brings work of a different kind:
A little world he feels, our man,
Brewing up in his brainpan,
He feels it start to move and live
And that he'd like it forth to give.

He'd have a true eye, shrewd enough,
And in himself sufficient love
To see things clear and see them plain,
And make them all his own again:
A fluent tongue he'd have also
To make the light and fine words flow;
In this the Muses joy might take,
A Meistersinger of him make.

Just now a woman young has crossed
The stoop, her body round, her breast
Ample, and her stance is strong,
Noble and straight she walks along,
Not wiggling with her skirt or ass,
Not ogling eyes to make a pass.
A measure in her hand she holds,
Her girdle ribbon all of gold,
Has on her head a barley wreath,
Bright as the day her eyes beneath;
Honour, she's called, or, if you will,
Magnanimity, or Skill.

Well, with fair greeting, in she comes;
He's not the least surprised, it seems,
So good, so beautiful, for sure,
He thinks, he's seen her oft before.

Says she: 'It's you that I have chosen,
From many in this world's confusion,
Clear senses and clear thoughts to have,
And nothing wicked to contrive.
When others criss and cross their ways,
You'll see all things with level gaze;
When others pitiably mope and groan,
You'll do your bit in a jesting tone;
On right and wrong you'll keep a watch,
Be plain direct in every touch,
Justice and virtue celebrate,
And naming evil name it straight.
Nothing softened or joked away,
No prettification, scribblers' play;
The world before you stand I bid
As it before Albrecht Dürer did:
Its vigorous masculinity,
Its inner strength and constancy.
Nature's genius by your hand
Will lead you then through every land,
Show you this life, just as it is,
People, their strange activities,
Muddling, questing, hitting, driving,
Pushing, pulling, crowding, chafing;
This world, its razzling dazzling leaps,
Boom and crash in its ant heaps;
May this no more affect you, though,
Than might a magic picture show.
For people on earth you'll write it down,
As a work of wit that must be known.'
Then opened she his window wide,
Showed him the motley throng outside,
Under the sky, such various folks
As you may read of in his books.

As our dear master now delights
In viewing Nature and her sights,

88

You see upon the other side
An ancient dame toward him glide;
She's called by all Historia,
Mythologia, Fabula;
With rickety gasping steps she brings
An enormous board, with woodcuttings:
God the Father you see, all cuffs and folds,
As he a class in Scripture holds,
Adam and Eve, Paradise, the Snake,
Sodom and Gomorrah hit by earthquake;
The Twelve Distinguished Women see upon a
Looking Glass of Dignity and Honour;
Then bloodlust galore, murder, sacrilege,
The Tyrants Twelve on their rampage,
Instruction, too, and counsel, are descried,
You see Saint Peter, with his Goat, unsatisfied
With all the world and its regime:
You see Our Lord reproving him.
Pictures, too, adorn her dress,
On hem and train, an ample space,
Of worldly vice and virtue tales:
All this our master's sight regales,
And wonderfully pleased he is,
He makes it all his business.
Thence he will make palpable
Whatever he takes, in parable
And true instruction, telling no lies,
As if it played before his eyes.
His wits by this were so spellbound
He never would have turned around,
Had he not heard behind his back
Bells and clappers ping and clack.
Then was he of a Fool aware,
With goatish leaps amonkeying there,
Doing for him with farce and folly
An interlude, all blithe and jolly.
Behind him on a rope this fool
Drags all the others, big and small,
The tall, the crooked, the thin, the fat,
All crack-witted, and dumb at that.
With an oxtail whip he them commands
Like a troop of monkeys doing a dance:

Bids them go bathe, scoffs at their shapes,
Cuts them to see the worm escapes,
Complaining the while, with bitterness,
That never their number grows the less.

Now round he looks and round, enough
Nearly to twist his noddle off:
Where should he find words for it all?
Where, to connect, the wherewithal?
How shall he keep his spirit strong
For writing of it, or for song?
Then from a fringe of cloud apace
Descends, through a top window space,
The Muse, most holy to behold,
Like Our Lady, framed in gold.
Round him now she puts a ring
Of light – truth, strong and everlasting.
'I consecrate you now,' she says,
'For that I come, and you to bless.
There burns in you a holy flame:
Exalt it into light sublime.
But that the life which is your spur
May delicate remain and pure,
A balm and nourishment I have put
Into your being's very root,
So may delight your soul imbue
As does the bud the morning dew.'

Then, secretly, a way she shows
Out through the back door of the house,
And in the sheltered garden sitting
A lovely girl, for someone waiting,
Near the elder, by a brook:
She hardly gives the world a look,
Her head is bowed, downcast her eye,
She sits beneath an apple tree,
And from her lap fresh roses takes,
Of bud and leaf a garland makes
With nimble fingers, skilfully.
For whom might now this garland be?
Her self-attentive curves attest
That breath of hope now swells her breast;

So many dreams in her aspire,
She does not know what to desire;
So many moods are passing by,
Sometimes she cannot help but sigh.
Wherefore, my dear, this darkish brow?
What weighs upon you is not so
But full of lightsome joy and bliss
That now, for you, full ready is
In one for whom you'll mitigate,
Just with a look, the snarls of fate,
And who must needs be born anew
With every wondrous kiss from you.
Holds he your slender body tight,
From every toil he'll find respite;
Into your rounded arms he'll sink,
There freshest life and vigour drink.
Sweet youth to you will too come back
With merriness that now you lack.
Your teasing wit will sometimes bite,
Or, roguish sometimes, him delight:
So love will never then grow old
And never he, the poet, cold.

Now secret joys are his to have,
Come floating from a cloud above
Evergreen oakleaves, garlanded:
Therewith Posterity wreathes his head;
Such folks into the frog pond pitch
As gave for their master never a stitch.

1776

GÜNTER KUNERT

Dürer's 'Hieronymus im Gehäuse'

In the foreground
a lion, prone, detached, a
tired one, without
eyes for anything, close
beside it

a dog snoozes, in
this perspective further off
sits the saint in the portrayed
stillness of his chamber,
at his desk

he is writing
who knows what, on
paper, it might be
the one thing
unthought of, the word

deluded
target fabricators
forgot, the word secreting
all it meant to take
shelter, safe

and sound
in the grey light that flows
without end
through these bullseye
windows

1980

BERTOLT BRECHT

Garden in Progress

High up above the Pacific coast, below it
The quiet thunder of waves, the rumble of oil trucks,
Lies the garden of the actor.

The white house is shaded by gigantic eucalyptus trees,
Dusty remains of the Mission that has vanished.
No other trace of it, except perhaps the Indian
Granite snake's head, there beside the well
As if expecting, patiently,
Several civilisations to collapse.

And on a block of wood there was a Mexican sculpture
In porous tufa, a child with wicked eyelids:
Behind it the bricks of the work shed.
A fine grey bench as in a Chinese drawing
Faced the work shed. Sitting there, having a talk,
You look over your shoulder at the lemon grove,
Effortless.

In a secret balance the parts
Are resting or vibrant, yet nowhere
Do they escape the delighted gaze, and the master hand
Of the ubiquitous gardener permits no unit
Sheer singularity: among the fuchsias, say,
A cactus might be growing. Also the seasons
Steadily order the insertions of sight; the clusters
Flower or fade, now here, now there. A lifetime
Would not suffice to comprehend it all. Yet,
As the garden grew to a plan,
The plan grew with the garden.

The robust oaks on the princely lawn
Are palpable creations of fantasy. The garden's master
Constructs with a sharp saw,
Year by year, new networks of branches.

Yet ignored grass rankles behind the hedge
Around the giant wild rose bush. Zinnias and bright
Convolvulus float over the incline. Sweet peas and ferns
Sprout around the stack of firewood.

In the corner beneath the spruce
You'll find, by the wall, the fuchsia garden. Like immigrants
The lovely plants, oblivious of their provenance,
Astonish one another with daring reds –
The fuller flowers surround the little native
Delicate and strong shrub with its tiny calices.

And there was a garden inside the garden,
Under a fir, so in the shade,
Ten feet wide and twelve feet long,
It was as large as a park,
With a little moss and cyclamen
And two clumps of camellias.

And not only with his own plants and trees
Did the master of the garden construct, but also
With plants and trees of his neighbours; told of this
He confessed with a smile: I steal from everywhere.
(But the bad things he concealed
With his own plants and trees.)

Dispersed in all directions
Stood small bushes, thoughts of a night;
Wherever one went, so long as one looked,
One found a sketch with life secreted in it.

Past the house a monastic lane of hibiscus leads,
Densely planted, so on a promenade
One has to bend them back, releasing thus
The full fragrance of their blossoms.

In the monastic lane by the house, beside the lamp,
Is planted the Arizona cactus, tall as a man, which flowers
Every year for a single night, this year
To the thunder of gunfire from ships at their manoeuvres,
With white flowers big as fists, subtle
As a Chinese actor.

Unhappily the lovely garden, high above the coast,
Is built on friable rock. Landslides take,
Without warning, suddenly whole sections into the depths.
Apparently
Not much time is left in which to finish it.

1945

GUILLAUME APOLLINAIRE

The Palace of Thunder

The outlet open on the trench in chalk
You see the opposite wall which looks like nougat
And the wet deserted corridor forking left and right
Where a shovel dies prostrate with a startled face
     two regulation eyes fixing it under the lockers
A rat retreats in a hurry as I advance in a hurry
And the trench runs off crowned with chalk
     and sprinkled with branches
Like a white hollow phantom putting a void wherever it goes

And aloft the roof is blue and quite covers the gaze
     enclosed by several straight lines
But this side of the outlet is the palace quite new
     although it seems to be ancient
The ceiling is built of railroad ties
Between them bits of chalk and tufts of pine needles
And from time to time chalk débris drops
     like bits of age
Beside the outlet closed by floppy cloth of the kind
     commonly used for packaging
There is a hole for a hearth and what burns there
     is like a fire in the soul
It whirls with such turbulence and clings fast to
     what it devours and is so fugitive

Taut wires everywhere serve as a frame to support planks
Also forming hooks and from them one suspends
     a thousand things
As from memory
Blue sacks blue caps blue scarves blue tunics
Pieces of sky tissues of purest memory
And sometimes in the air vague clouds of chalk
     are floating

On the plank are gleaming fuses detonators goldwashed
     jewels with enamelled heads
Black and white and red

Ropedancers awaiting their turn to move into the trajectories
An inconspicuous elegant ornament for this
        subterranean dwelling
Which six beds in a horseshoe embellish
Six beds covered with rich blue overcoats

On top of the palace a high chalk tumulus
And plaques of corrugated iron
Static river of this ideal domain
But dry for all that flows is the fire gushing
        out of melinite
The flower park of cartridge caps gushes out of
        sloping holes
Lots of bells with soft tones of glittering
        cartridge cases
Elegant and small pine trees of a Japanese landscape

Sometimes the palace is lit by a candle flame
        no bigger than a mouse
O tiny palace seen as through the wrong end of a telescope
Little palace where all is muted
Little palace where all is new nothing old
And where all is precious everyone clad like a king
In the corner a saddle mounted on a box
A daily paper drags along the ground

And yet in this new dwelling all seems old
So distinctly one is aware that the love of antiquity
A taste for the antiquail
Must have come to men at the time of the caverns
Everything was so precious and new
Everything is so precious and new
That anything older or used there seems to be
                More precious by far
Than what is at hand
In this palace dug underground in the chalk so white
        and new
And two fresh cut steps
                Not two weeks old
Are so old and so used in this palace which seems antique
        but does not imitate antiquity

One sees whatever is more simple more new and
      whatever is
Nearest to antique beauty so-called
And anything heavy with ornament
Needs must age to have the beauty they call antique
Beauty which is the nobility the force ardour soul
      the abundance
Of what is new and useful
Above all if it is simple simple
As simple as the little palace of thunder

1918

IBN ZAMRAK

The Alhambra Inscription

I am a garden graced by every beauty:
See my splendour, then you will know my being.
For Mohammad, my king, and in his name
The noblest things, past or to come, I equal:
Of me, a work sublime, Fortune desires
That I outshine all other monuments.
What pleasure I provide for eyes to see!
In me, any noble man will take fresh heart:
Like an amulet the Pleiades protect him,
The magic of the breeze is his defender.
A shining dome, peerless, here displays
Evident splendours and more secret ones.
Gemini extends to it a touching hand,
Moon comes to parley, stars clustering there
Turn no longer in the sky's blue wheel:
In the two courts, submissively, they linger
To be of service to their lord, like slaves.
It is no marvel that the stars should err,
Moving across their marks and boundaries,
And are disposed to serve my sovereign lord,
Since all who serve him glory in his glory.
The palace portico, so beautiful
It bids to rival heaven's very vault;
Clothed in a woven raiment fine as this
You can forget the busy looms of Yemen.
See what arches mount upon its roof
And spring from columns burnished by the light
Like the celestial spheres that turn and turn
Above the luminous column of the dawn.
Altogether the columns are so beautiful
That every tongue is telling their renown;
Black the shadow-darkened cornice cuts
Across the fair light thrown by snowy marble;
Such opalescent shimmers swarm about,
You'd say, for all their size, they are of pearl.
Never have we seen a palace rise so high,
With such a clarity, such expanse of outline;

Never did a garden brim like this with flowers,
Fruits more sweet to taste or more perfumed.
It pays the fee required of beauty's critic
Twice and in two varieties of coin:
For if, at dawn, an early breeze will toss
Into his hands drachmas of light galore,
Later, in the thick of tree and shrub,
With coins of gold the sun will lavish him.
What sired these kindred things? A victory:
Still none can match the lineage of the king.

14th century

JOHANN WOLFGANG VON GOETHE

A Thousand Forms

Take on a thousand forms, hide as you will,
O Most-Beloved, at once I know tis you;
Conceal yourself in magic veils, and still,
Presence-in-All, at once I know tis you.

The cypress thrusting artless up and young,
Beauty-in-Every-Limb, I know tis you;
The channelled crystal wave life flows along,
All-Gentling-Tender-One, I know tis you.

You in the fountain plume's unfolding tip,
All-Playful-One, what joy to know tis you;
Where cloud assumes a shape and changes it,
One-Manifold-in-All, I know tis you.

I know, when flowers veil the meadow ground,
O Starry-Twinkle-Hued, in beauty you;
When thousand-armed the ivy gropes around,
Environer-of-All, I know tis you.

When on a mountain sparks of dawn appear,
At once, Great Gladdener, I welcome you;
Then with a sky above rotund and clear,
Then, Opener-of-the-Heart, do I breathe you.

What with bodily sense and soul I know,
Teacher-of-All, I know alone through you;
All hundred names on Allah I bestow,
With each will echo then a name for you.

1815

Sestina with Ship Hoist

Go to it, wits. Honeycomb bottlejuice (praydough to 'Orion, his shoulder') – cinnamon ampule, swallowtongue, aintmeanthood Follywood.

Doppler androgyne. How does thought come to pass. How do I go.

By the be-coming of every context, let's say, by the driving force of the sestina formula 6-1-5-2-4-3 ('the six things – to be taken in, near enough, at a glance'; anthropomorphic event, a synoptic molecular magnitude).

Eccenters, Dryads, Doremisolifications.

The sestina then: in literary-historical terms that lyric species which arose around AD 1200 in troubadour poetry with Arnaut Daniel (who also set the strophes in a melodic continuum) and via Dante and Petrarch, via Spain, Portugal, France, England, German Baroque and Romanticism (scantly, scantly, but still . . .), then again via Ezra Pound, W.H. Auden, Ungaretti, Rudolf Borchardt, Joan Brossa, Ernst Krenek (a composer like the troubadour) has persisted into our times – we might mention Ron Padgett, Elizabeth Bishop, the OULIPO writers and all the literalist performers who continue to play in the little tradition of large possibilities.[1]

All in all: six six-line strophes and a three-line coda, thus 6 x 6 + 3 = 39 lines, a poem of medium length. Which rhymes, of course – but how? For 39 lines only 6 rhyme-words are available (entire rhyme *words*, that is, placed at line-ends), which are repeated from strophe to strophe – and to that end the sestina excogitated a rhythm of its own (one might call it an embrace that 'lets go', or an embrace that's 'cracking'): from the first 1-2-3-4-5-6 derives the series 6-1-5-2-4-3, and so on, from strophe to strophe.

On 16 June 1991, we go – Emily Böhme, Harry Mathews, Marianne Frisch, the Wichners, and myself – to the ship hoist at Niederfinow, near Eberswalde, about 70 km north-east of Berlin.[2]

A splendid technical construction, towering unadorned in the landscape, and extant from the Bauhaus era. And still in operation.

I read the technical details from the back of the admission ticket:

> Date & cost of construction: 1927-34; 27.5 Mill. RM.
> Hoist Frame: 94 m. long, 27 m. wide, 60 m. high.
> Trough: 85 m. long, 12 m. wide, 2.50 m. deep.

Weight when flooded: 4300 tons.
Hoisting altitude: 36 m.
Hoist duration at 12 cm. per second: 5 mins.
Sluice duration: 20 mins.
Counterweights: 4300 tons, connected to trough by 256 steel
cables of 52 mm. diameter. The cables run over pulleys
of 3.50 m. diameter, each weighing c. 5 tons.
Power source: 4 electric motors, each of 55 kw. raise and lower
the trough by rack and pinion.
Slab: steel-reinforced concrete 20 m. deep. The base plate is
4 m. thick.

And I know: there should be, no, there must be, a sestina in this. For days the material proposes itself.

It all clicked when I looked at the bookshelves – Jean Paul, *Titan*, Vol. I: that finally precipitated the sestina, as the sestina had precipitated the click.

There, on pages 94, 27, and 60 (corresponding to the measurements of the construction in metres) I found the rest of the language material:[3]

sestina with ship hoist

now let us all keenly see for the duration of a hoist
at a torture soupé the two biographical courts
put together; and dancing in, the trough
94 long, 60 high, 27 wide, on a bed
with twelvefold girdles, from one to another dash
low metre mountain music in a powder mantle

the storm locked in a coach in a powder mantle
loses by this bandaging of his eyes with the hoist's
downfallen locks a vast deal; how the dash
lays on – long counterweights, linked by courts
with 4300 tons of water minutes, guess the bed
of black cold worldlings – epicurism in the trough

stands not the giant there like micromegas in the trough
of the body politic? seized was he by the powder mantle
steel-reinforced towering over a bed
just as high, just as stiff and stark? the hoist's
slab duration is five natures flat over the courts
leaf by leaf, its long dash

103

to bind on the old taffeta ribbon – dash –
and prink for all maybeings the ship trough
by rack and pinion, milliomillio's courts –
the very name Rack opened a powder mantle
to him like a melon under its bell of the hoist
the child grew full of love on a bed

22 mm. thick as a leader in the dance from one bed
to another, the power source was for him a dash;
where the wheat ear and the cluster and the olive hoist
often as if together raise on a pulley the trough
and lower it, one sees there the powder mantle
crumble 36 metres deep, over swelling courts

the dangerous bird-pole of these artificial courts
dancing in – and don't you see there the bed
of the sluice altitude robed in a powder mantle?
that he thus guessed the tulip tree's sparkling dash
with fifty-five baptismal and funeral bells per trough
and Borromean books before the lace mask of a hoist

how beautiful, and then the bandage of the hoist
seized him 86 m. long overwhelming wide and with the trough
through 256 steel cables and a rack per dash.

Amazingly – at least for me – this sestina, in which not a word came
from me, might simply be a Poem of Unification. Of German
Unification, too.

But if such an interpretive wake occurs, perhaps already at the out-
set of writing, it is sprayed over the entire development, almost against
the grain of thought – pigeon's eggs, goose eggs, cuckoo's eggs in both
word-fields (on the one hand technical data, Jean Paul on the other)
succeed one another, mingle with one another, crinkle the syntax 'from
one bed to another', thus activate 'artificial courts', the trough becomes
a wake, the powder mantle of the politicians in the 'mask' before they
appear on television drops with feathers ruffled into the make-up pot
– pressure of fact and accessories accomplish something that now
seems to me really datable, at an event irreversible, and incisive, with
'256 steel cables and a rack per dash'.

Have I been considering, I now consider, the compelling way in
which the two material courts coalesce in the sestina and *had* to be
spun together – or was the hoist of union a pre-meditated affair, as with

Schiller, who only had to interpret it choicely? Amazingly, in any case, the 'joint intent' was already poetological, just as history was.

– or, to run a loop here, simply internalize, where what and who is when thought occurs as event, as enaction of possibilities: the sestina really might, ah, I ask you, be something like an analogical model for the occurrence of thought in the head when thoughts are being thought – Sigma of a linguistically unsaturated process of making.

Thus a phantom system.

Thought, the way it re-fers to itself, envoids itself.

Isomorphic rejection in this rocking-chair: linguistically the sestina would be one language among many.

From the standpoint of experimental physics, thus of a test result, it might be a little generative machine, a truth drug, a philosopher's kohinoor, an Oulipotential.

From the standpoint of sociology and medicine, probably a tuberous death-cup.

From the standpoint of trees a cast shadow, from the standpoint of seaweed a jellyfish.

A virtual according-to-circumstantiality.

For, considered anamorphotically (as something through the inner-outer mirror of a Möbius strip), the sestina might be, *in effigie*, slow motion, or more specifically, a space-condenser in action – a thing and a non-thing in one.

Six-One-Five-Two-Four-Three: I think I'm describing a thought-paradigm around which a vegetable stroking and a flesh creeping happen.

1991–2

---

1.   – and we might also mention, quite a discovery, Pierre Lartigue's recent anthology (with a richly documented essay), *Le hélice d'écrire: La sestine*. Paris: Les belles lettres, 1994. (Translator's note: OULIPO – a post-Pataphysical group of experimental writers formed in France during the 1960s.)

2.   Translator's note: the ship hoist is not just a lock; a ship on one canal-water level is lowered or raised, with the trough it floats in, by a powerful rack and pinion crane, to the next canal.

3.   Translator's note: The English version derives from Charles Brooks's translation of 1877 (Henry Holt).

KURT SCHWITTERS

The Dadarotator

The dadarotator is intended personally for you. It is a peculiar combi-
nation of rotators, axes, and pistons, built with cadavers, nitric acid,
and Merz in such a way that you enter it with complete understanding
and emerge from it with none. This has great advantages for you. Invest
your money in a dadarotator cure, you'll never regret it, after the treat-
ment you'll never be able to regret anything. Rich or poor, whichever
you are, it's all the same, the dadarotator frees you even from money
per se. As a capitalist you go into the funnel, pass through several
pistons, and plunge into acid. Then you come into contact with a
corpse or two. Vinegar dribbles cubism dada. Then you get to see the
Great Rotatory Dada. (Not the President of the Universe, as many sup-
pose.) The dadarotator beams with wit and is pronged with about
100,000 needlepoints. After you've been flung back and forth, someone
will read you my latest poems, until you collapse in a faint. Then comes
the fulling and dadarotating, and suddenly there you are, with a fresh
haircut, out in the open, an antibourgeois. Before the treatment the eye
of the needle horrifies you, after it nothing can. You'll be a rotarydada
and you'll pray to the machine like someone inspired. – Amen.

c. 1922

4. HUMAN FIGURES

ABU JAFAR AHMAD IBN SA'ID

The Procuress

The procuress, said to be a bad lot
        and she's proud of it
More close than night a man on the road
        she'll hug a secret
Tiptoes into anyone's home,
        how far inside, nobody knows
Polite, with a nod for everyone
        and a kind word along with it
Back and forth she scuttles,
        no bother to folks next door
Never a second to fold her cloak,
        it outflaps any battle flag
Can tell a crime from a crafty trick
        so long as she finds it useful to
No idea where the mosque is
        but knows the taverns inside out
Forever smiling, very devout,
        jokes and tales up every sleeve
Arithmetic at her fingertips,
        abracadabras, horoscopes
Never a cent for shoes of her own
        but well-off where most are not
Her palaver so smooth
        she'd matchmake water and fire in a wink.

12th century

EDUARD MÖRIKE

Johann Kepler

Last night lying in bed as I looked at the eastern star,
    Taking a good long look, that star with the reddish light,
And thought of the man who, being impelled by the god,
    Bowed to the heavenly task of calculating its course,
And who endeavoured with steadfast work to dull and despise
    Poverty's terrible sting, though the endeavour was vain:
My heart blazed with bitter grief and, ah, master, I thought,
    Was this fate of yours all that the gods could give?
Homer exalted Achilles, stirred by his noble and godlike
    Grandeur, and poets do choose them a hero in song,
Likewise upon that star you turned all the force of your mind
    And its tremendous course was your eternal theme.
Yet a song's not the thing that occasions a god to flutter
    Down from his golden throne, bringing deliverance
For a man to whom dark days the loftier power has ordained,
    And you stars up there, never touched by a human fate,
Over the heads of the wise and foolish blithely you move
    Eternally calm as you pass unperturbed on your ways.

1838

ALFRED VAGTS

A Farmhand
(† November 3, 1917)

I settled beside him as into a church pew,
this stall his legacy, himself long mute
though the animal choir sang out, the chorale
of thin high voices detectible in flowers
when bees hushed into them, in the poppies
between his brown fists peeping like holycards,
mementos of our pilgrimage through blood,
out of an old prayer-book's dull gold trim.
The sky hung from golden solar rings
and ballooned a little, a blue curtain
with swallows being woven into it;
God behind it
whispered to his son as he went earthward –
our shuddering his Passion Story.
Wind motioned blessing to the lowly grasses
and we too bowed our heads to it;
of blessing done, in peace,
oat stalks whispered round a boundary stone.
Ridges razed, blown away,
weeds were ravaging the fields
whose borders meant the oldest rule for him.
A plough, stuck fast, derelict like his own,
lightly he touched it, still too soon,
yet prophesying: Come the day, from here
ploughs will measure out the earth anew.
He stroked the scant rye sprouting wild,
as if the mowing should begin tomorrow.
Today the senseless work was war:
the farmhand must toil, year in, year out;
none but the few off-duty days for his own field;
masters' names unchanged – Lord Miles of Muck –
the same as in the Peasants' War, before and since.
Die for that? (The mujik lifts his daystar fist.)
He moved his mouth to chew on death, one grain,
wearily spat it out, tasted too late,

111

ergot, black with blight, and let himself die.
The hand he held out, skyward, cupped
as when feeding his brown horse a hunk of bread,
some scraps of clay had trickled into it.

1920

OKTAY RIFAT

The Housemaids

Fastidious women they were,
their beds dreamily bathed in white,
their picture-bird scrawls chirping tweet-tweet,
they were clear water, tiled roof,
a tinkling bell, children amazingly alive,
like sun parlours they watched the perch fishermen
turn the sea into a field of light,
sensitive, nocturnal, the struts
to prop their houses green, burnished their trays
with ash and lemon,
sorrowful eyes in which a dead man lay
waiting to rise again in a room of theirs,
into their bags they stuffed the earth
of testimonials, to trickle it out
in a far country they reached by steamboat,
a treasure, every one of them, these housemaids,
sunlight striking a jeweller's windowpane.

1984

IBN AZ-ZAQQAQ

Drunken Beauty

Her beauty, luminous and singular,
The carefree splendour of it made my day.
She gave me wine to drink: it was her mouth
Intoxicated me. The crystal held
Ambrosia, her lips their pearls;
Glistening liquid.
Her rosy cheeks gave off an airy glow,
I kissed and kissed them, till, the frenzy over,
She was a slender branch the breeze has bent;
I gave my shoulder to her for a pillow,
My arms around her held the surge of dawn.

Early 12th century

FRIEDERIKE MAYRÖCKER

Depression

my mother tells me
she met at the grocer's
an old
schoolfriend, seventy-four, the same age,
asked how's it going she
had shouted: Pull
the blanket up, over your head,
see nowt, hear nowt!

1982

KARIN KIWUS

Alienation through Work

To me it really makes no difference
    helping you in the kitchen
        but sometimes now I miss
    these hesitant half-moments
leaning against the doorpost and looking at you
    the way you put a breakfast together
        with your whole body

You always measured out the tea
    pinch by pinch
        in the hollow of your left hand
and with your teeth
    tore a packet of sliced cheese open
the frigidaire door
    you shut with your thigh
and crushed the bulky egg cartons
    with your wooden soled shoes

You always pushed with your elbow
    saucepans off the cooker top
and placed others on it, hardly to be lifted
    with both hands

You always had these pan handles
    in one hand
        and a cookie in the other
and a cloth slipping off your shoulder
    when any liquid spilled on the floor
and you with bare toes
    pulled a floorcloth out and wiped it up
as if a lathe were underneath your foot

And puffcheeked like a sleepy angel
    with a slightly distant look
        you always blew on the boiling milk
and the five-minute eggs you put
    hot into the breast pocket of your bathrobe

It was always such a relief
    to notice how with complete confidence
        you could take a hold on anything in the mornings
self-oblivious and with an agility
    which made me feel at one with you
        at first sight

Now when I stand beside you in the kitchen
    and in my own way
        attentively cope with things
I no longer have my eyes on you
And since we really began to be together
    I have stopped feeling deep down
        how it really is
    when you and I begin a day

I am closer to you perhaps
    but you are always
        half an hour
            ahead of me now

1976

FEDERICO GARCÍA LORCA

Tamar and Amnon

The moon circles in the sky
over the parching lands,
while the summer sows
murmurs of tiger and flame.
Above the roof tops
metal nerves were sounding.
Curly gusts of air
came with the bleating of wool.
Earth offers herself
seething with scars,
or shivering with sharp
cauteries of white lights.

Tamar dreamed –
birds in her throat –
to the sound of cold tambourines
and moon zithers.
Her nakedness in the roof angle –
sharp polestar of palm –
asks of her belly snow
and hail of her spine.
Tamar sang
naked on the terrace.
Around her feet
five doves of ice.
Amnon, slim and sharp,
looked at her from the tower,
his groin full of foam,
of tremors his face.
His bright nakedness
stretched on the terrace,
between his teeth the murmur
of an arrow that has struck.
Amnon was looking
at the round low moon,
and he saw in the moon the hard
hard breasts of his sister.

Amnon at half past three
lay down on the bed.
The whole room was a torment
under his wing-brimming gaze.
Burnished sand, massive light
buries villages under it,
or reveals a fleeting
coral of rose and dahlia.
The well's crushed liquid
breeds silence in jars.
On mossy boles
the taut cobra sings.
Amnon moans in bed
over cool cool sheets.
Ivy of shuddering swarms
over his burned flesh.
Silent Tamar entered
the silence of the room,
all hue of vein and Danube
darkened by distant touches.
– Tamar, blanket my gaze
with your absolute dawn.
The threads of my blood weave
frills for your skirt.
– Brother, let me go.
Your kisses on my spine
are wasps and little winds
in double swarms of flutes.
– Tamar, in your high breasts
two fishes call to me,
in the penfold of your fingertips
the murmur of a rose.

The king's one hundred horses
were neighing in the bailey.
Slenderness of the vine
withstood bucketed sun.
Now he grabs her by the hair,
now he rips her blouse.
Warm corals draw
streams on a blond map.

O what shrieks were heard
high above the houses!
What thickness of knives
and tunics torn to pieces.
By the sad staircases
slaves rush up and down.
Pistons and thighs work
under clouds that stopped.
Around Tamar they howl,
the virgin gipsies,
others collect the drops
of her martyred flower.
White linen turns crimson
in locked bedrooms.
Fishes and vines exchanged
murmurs of cool dawn.

In a rage the violator
Amnon flees on his mare.
Negroes shoot arrows at him
from walls and lookouts.
And when the four hoof beats
were four vibrations only,
David took a pair of shears,
and cut the strings of his harp.

1928

EDUARD MÖRIKE

Erinna to Sappho

'Manifold are the paths to Hades,' says an
Old song – 'and one of them will be yours to walk,
Have no doubt of it!' Who, Sappho sweetest, doubts it?
Doesn't each day say the same?
But the living aren't likely to take such a saying
Heavily to heart, and the fisherman down by the sea
From childhood on, he hardly hears the wavebeat falling.
– Yet strangely my heart took fright today. Listen!

Early sunlight in the garden
Circling the tops of trees
Enticed this lazybones (not long ago that's what you called me)
Out of my sultry bed betimes.
I felt at peace; but through my veins
The blood pulsed fitfully, and my cheeks were pale.

Then as I unloosed my braids at the dressing table,
And with my scented comb parted in front the hanging
Veil of hair – a strange meeting of eyes occurred in the mirror.
Eyes, I said, what can it be you want of me?
Spirit of mine, you're safe at home in there today,
Faithfully wed to living senses,
As with a serious look, to put me off, half smiling, a demon now,
You nod at me and prophesy death!
– Ha! then the shiver pierced me
Like lightning! as if a deadly blackflighted arrow
Shot past hardly missing my head,
And covering my face with my hands I sat there a long time,
Staring down amazed into the dizzying dark abyss.

And I pondered my own death;
Dry-eyed at first,
Until my thoughts turned, Sappho, to you
And to all my friends
And the graceful art of the Muses,
It was then the flood of tears came.

There, gleaming on the table, I saw your gift, the beautiful hairnet,
Fine fabric of Byssos, swarming with little golden bees.
This, when next we celebrate the flowery feast
Of Demeter's sovereign daughter,
I wish to consecrate to her, on my behalf and yours;
That she may favour us (for she is powerful),
That you may not need to shear too soon from your beloved head
The brown curl, in mourning for Erinna.

1864

Erinna, a highly esteemed young poetess of Greek antiquity, was a friend
and pupil of Sappho's around 600 BC. She died when she was nineteen.
Her most famous work was an epic, *The Spindle*, of which only the title is
known. Of her work, indeed, only some fragments of a few lines and three
epigrams have survived. Two statues were erected to her, and the Greek
anthology contains several epigrams by various authors in praise of her.

[Mörike's own prefatory note]

STÉPHANE MALLARMÉ

The Jinx

Above the stupefied herd of human beings,
Beggars of the Blue, their savage
Manes sprang out in flashes,
Their feet were on our paths.

Black wind unfurled its banners, whipped
Their march, a penetrating
Wind so cold, into their flesh
It etched irritant furrows.

Always in hope of happening on the sea,
Without bread or staves or
Urns they travelled, sank their teeth
In the golden lemon, bitter ideal.

Most expired, croaked in dark ravines,
Intoxicated with a joy to see
Their blood was flowing; Oh
Death – on their mute mouths the only kiss.

Their defeat, by a most puissant angel
Erect on the horizon,
Naked as his sword, scales
On his recognizant breast congealed a crimson.

They suck at sorrow as they sucked the dream,
And when they move to the drum-
Beat of voluptuous tears,
The populace kneels, their mother rises up.

They are consoled, resolute, majestic;
Yet in their tracks they drag
A hundred brothers, mocked
Ridiculous martyrs to the twists of hazard.

Gnaws on their sweet cheek a weeping salt,
Ashes they eat with the selfsame
Love, but low or farcical
The fate whose wheel they are broken on.

Peers of Prometheus, without his vulture,
They can excite,
As a drum excites, the slavish
Pity of peoples dull of tongue.

No, dismal, haunting a desert devoid of wells
They run beneath the lash
Of a mad monarch, the Jinx,
Who flattens them with the shock of his laughter.

He jumps up to ride threesome, sharing coupled lovers,
Then, the torrent crossed,
Into a pond he topples you, leaving
White swimmers changed into a lump of mud.

His doing – someone blows his bizarre last trump,
And children, fist in ass,
Aping his fanfare,
Will twist us into a laugh we can't stop.

His doing – if an urn adorns a wilted breast
With a rose, nubile,
Illumined afresh,
Drool will gleam on his damned bouquet.

And this dwarf skeleton coiffed with feathered felt
And booted, worms for real
Hair in its armpits, signifies
For them a vast, a sour infinitude.

Hurt, they'll provoke, or not, the pervert,
Their rasping rapier
Follows the beam of the moon,
To snow on his carcass and penetrate it.

Apologetic, bereft of the pride that sanctifies
Ill fortune, sad to wreak revenge,
With beaks pecking, on their bones,
They hanker for hatred, not for pique.

They are the sport of fiddlestring scrapers,
Guttersnipes, whores,
And the ancient mob of dragworms
Capering after the jug runs dry.

Poets good for a handout or revenge,
Ignorant of the evil in these gods
With faceless features,
Say they're a sorry lot, who've got no brains:

'They can run off, done with every exploit,
Like a filly escaping
The froth of a tempest,
Rather than gallop away wearing a breastplate.

'We'll make the victor drunk with incense at the feast,
But these buffoons,
Why not dress them up
In scarlet threads, howling for them to stop?'

When all disdainfully have spat on them,
Zeroes, beards that pray
Muttering to the thunderbolt,
These heroes, wasted by malign diseases, go

Hang themselves, ridiculous, from a lamppost.

1862–3 (?)

GERTRUD KOLMAR

The Old Woman

Today I'm ill, only today, tomorrow I'll be well.
Today I'm poor, only today, tomorrow I'll be rich.
But some day I shall always sit like this,
Shrinking icy into a sombre shawl, with a dry hacking cough,
Shuffle slow when I walk, and put bony hands to the fire.
Then I shall be old.

My hair's dark blackbird wings are grey,
My lips fusty withered blossoms,
And my body knows no longer the rise and fall of the red springing
    fountain of the blood.
I died perhaps
Long before my death.

And yet I was young.
Was loved by, went with a man, like nourishing brown bread in his
    hungry hand,
Was sweet as solacing drink to his thirsty mouth.
I smiled,
And the soft fleshy snakes of my arms allured, clinging in magical
    woodlands.
Smokeblue wings grew from my shoulders,
And I lay on his broader breast,
A white stream spilled murmuring down from the heart of the fir-crag.

But the day came and the moment came
When the bitter corn stood ripe that I had to harvest.
And the sickle cut my soul.
'Go,' I said, 'Go, my dear!
Look, my hair's threaded with old woman's silver,
Evening mist moistens my cheek,
My flower wilts under frost, and shivers.

Furrows cross my face,
Black dykes through autumn pasture.
Go: for I love you, my love.'

Silent I took the gold crown from my head and I hid my face then.
He went,
And his homeless footsteps brought him for sure to another haven,
     under brighter eye-stars.

My eyes have gone dim and can hardly bring needle and cotton
     together.
My eyes water wearily under their heavy wrinkled red-rimmed lids.

Seldom
From my dull glance dawns now the faint far-ago shine
Of a summer day,
When my light frock flowed rustling through fields of cuckoo-flower,
And my desire hurled raptures of larksong into the open sky.

[Before 1943] 1955

STÉPHANE MALLARMÉ

The Old Clothes Merchant

The rapid glance you fire
Through me where I stood
Distances me from my attire
And godlike I go nude.

1889

GÜNTER KUNERT

Face to Face

 (for Wolfgang Koeppen)

Deus absconditus lives opposite
the English garden, close to heaven,
top floor. His door unbolted. Freely enter,
pilgrim from afar.
                         In the corridor, a sofa
rescued from a junk heap in the street,
and on the sofa Cerberus,
with black pelt and gentle jowls,
legacy from a tamed paganhood.

Then he appears, himself, and undisguised,
ill-shaven, image of the patriarch,
a sightless and bewildered smile –
the marks are unmistakeable.
Thick lenses substitute for eyes,
so he can better overlook us.
The feeble hand lifting to greet us
trembled in consequence
of lonesome nights, many drinks.

Hardly had he noticed us, a call rang out,
human, desperate, a local call,
a telephonic De Profundis.
                         God hung up,
so as to act as if, by his
observance, pious, of caprice,
every one of us had been created,
with power and perseverance, equal.

1996

HEINZ PIONTEK

The Dispersion

We have the wind under our feet.
We have the wind at our backs.

Our neighbour's voice caught in the nets of snow.
So we crammed silver and bread into bags, unbolted the door.
As the night began to flicker, unarmed we ran to the stables,
and out onto roads where rat-hordes wandered.

Dented metal and the cold: the land of the defeated.
We inched along. A girl had a baby
between the wheels. A blind man stumbled, drawn on a string
behind people, and called through the snow: Where are we?

We must wait before we come to the crossroads.
We do not possess any documents.

Some died cowering – squabbling over dead horses;
some stretched out under canvas and spoke no more.
And as we passed singly over a smashed bridge,
many could be seen in the ice, as if they hung there.

The sky a sieve, and behind the column
of rack-wagons and coaches, all was silent,
a chill horizon, where we had bivouacked, someone asleep
frozen stiff and not afraid of pursuers now.

We may not light any fires.
We may not leave the convoy without permission.

They said to me: 'Tell us! We know too little about the people
who set out in the April of a pious century to establish –
twelve hundred perch of wilderness – their kingdoms;
and about the powder of bones in our graveyards, tell us!'

I told them: There was a people that left home
for the promised land, and did not arrive, and perished. –
'Fool! They found it, sweet and barbarous among streams of water!
But now it is we who must seek out our original country.'

We bow our shoulders under easy burdens.
We feed upon birds and snowflakes.

Our swarms thinned and shadows they cast were lean.
We lost each other. The East – like a fiery legend –
collapsed behind armies. It was desolation
and a cloud of ash adrift over desert and dark as long ago.

But a man drew level, leading a boy, a man exhausted,
his tunic was singed by many summers,
he carried an old man, his father, limp on his shoulders.
Then we saw dawn breaking around us, with light as of rose petals.

We shall come to a sure city in the wind.
We shall find peace rooted in rock.

1955 (slight revisions 1990)

PAUL CELAN

Fugue of Death

Black milk of daybreak we drink it at nightfall
we drink it at noon in the morning we drink it at night
drink it and drink it
we are digging a grave in the sky is it ample to lie there
A man in the house he plays with the serpents he writes
he writes when the night falls to Germany your golden hair Margarete
he writes it and walks from the house the stars glitter he whistles his
    dogs up
he whistles his Jews out and orders a grave to be dug in the earth
he commands us now on with the dance

Black milk of daybreak we drink you at night
we drink in the morning at noon we drink you at nightfall
drink you and drink you
A man in the house he plays with the serpents he writes
he writes when the night falls to Germany your golden hair Margarete
Your ashen hair Shulamith we are digging a grave in the sky it is ample
    to lie there

He shouts stab deeper in earth you there you others you sing and you
    play
he grabs at the iron in his belt and swings it and blue are his eyes
stab deeper your spades you there and you others play on for the
    dancing

Black milk of daybreak we drink you at night
we drink you at noon in the morning we drink you at nightfall
drink you and drink you
a man in the house your golden hair Margarete
your ashen hair Shulamith he plays with the serpents

He shouts play sweeter death's music death comes as a master from
    Germany
he shouts stroke darker the strings and as smoke you shall climb to the
    sky
then you'll have a grave in the clouds it is ample to lie there

Black milk of daybreak we drink you at night
we drink you at noon death comes as a master from Germany
we drink you at nightfall and morning we drink you and drink you
a master from Germany death comes with eyes that are blue
with a bullet of lead he will hit in the mark he will hit you
a man in the house your golden hair Margarete
he hunts us down with his dogs in the sky he gives us a grave
he plays with the serpents and dreams death comes as a master from
    Germany

your golden hair Margarete
your ashen hair Shulamith

1945

5. FABLED FIGURES

The Unicorn

The peacocks' pride,
Blue, green and golden, flowered in the twilight
Of tropical overgrowth, of tree-top, and grey monkeys
Grinned, quarrelled, dangled and romped, scuffled among tendrils.
The great tiger crouched, flashed claws, stared, lay low
As the dumb bewildering beast flew through his Indian forests,
Westward to the sea.

The unicorn.

His hoofs beat the water,
Playful, lightly. Waves reared,
Exuberant,
And the unicorn ran with the whinnying, cavorting, chivvying silver-
maned herd.
Over them
Black storks flying wrote rapid enigmas on the sky of Arabia;
Sunset there, proffering a dish of fruit:
Pears yellow, and red apples,
Peach and orange and plump grape,
Slices of ripe melon.
Black cliffs smouldered in sundown,
Fortresses of amethyst,
Whitenesses glowed, enchanted castles of carnelian and topaz.

The rose mists hung late over the dovecoloured darkening waters of the
bay.

The unicorn.

His hoofbeats whirled the sand up,
Raising dust without sound. He saw
Lonely cities, pallid, with cupola and minaret,
Tombstones in graveyards, tranquil under a ringing moon,
He saw
Ruins, homes desolate, tenanted by ghosts, in glistening darkness,
Under cold constellations.

The desert owl enticed him once,
And distant jackals howled lamenting;
Hyenas laughed.
Under the date palm, at the tent door,
The white Syrian dromedary raised from dream his small head, and his
     bell tinkled.

Onward the unicorn, onward.

For his light flying feet came from afar in Golden Ophir,
And from his eyes glittered the gaze of snakes which the charmer's flute
     commands to rise from baskets, to sway and dance,
But the steep horn central upon his brow shed a light more tender,
     milky, shimmering
Over the bare hands and soft-veiled breasts of the woman
Who stood there,
Among the clumps of manna grass.

Her greeting:
Humbleness,
And the quiet radiance of deep awaiting eyes,
And a breathing, the mouth's faint murmur flowing. –
Fountain in night.

[Before 1943] 1955

Kaspar is Dead

alas our good kaspar is dead.

who'll now hide the burning flag in the cloudpigtail and every day cock a black snook.

who'll now turn the coffeegrinder in the primeval tub.

who'll now lure the idyllic doe from the petrified paperbag.

who'll now blow the noses of ships parapluis windudders beefathers ozonespindles and who'll bone the pyramids.

alas alas alas our good kaspar is dead. saint dingdong kaspar is dead.

the grass-shark rattles his teeth heartrendingly in the bellbarns when his forename is spoken, therefore I shall go on sighing his familyname kaspar kaspar kaspar.

why hast thou forsaken us. into what form has thy great beautiful soul migrated. hast thou become a star or a chain of water hanging from a hot whirlwind or an udder of black light or a transparent tile on the groaning drum of the rocky essence.

now our tops and toes go dry and the fairies are lying halfcharred on the funeral pyre.

now the black skittle alley thunders behind the sun and nobody winds up the compasses and the pushcart wheels any more.

who'll now eat with the phosphorescent rat at the lonely barefoot table.

who'll now shoo away the siroccoco devil when he tries to ravish the horses.

who'll now elucidate for us the monograms in the stars.

his bust will grace the mantelpieces of all truly noble men but that's no consolation and snuff for a death's head.

1920

HANS ARP

Baobab

And she gave birth to a strong healthy boy
who was named Baobab.
The boy grew and grew,
and did not stop growing
and grew as high as the blue of the sky itself.
Baobab's compatriots liked to look into the eyes
of whomsover they might be talking to.
But this was no longer possible in the case
of a person as tall as Baobab was.
So they lifted a lot of earth
and dug a chasmic hole,
into which Baobab willingly inserted himself,
for he too found it unbearable
not to be able to look into the eyes
of whomsover he might be talking to.
The earth they lifted
they threw over the edge of their small star
into the emptiness.
After Baobab had spent
a hundred years in this hole,
he began to disappear.
Every day he grew smaller and smaller,
till at length he disappeared altogether.
Now the inhabitants of the small star
were left with nothing but a chasmic hole
and a narrow strip of land around the hole,
and they looked alternately
into the chasmic hole on their small star
and over the edge of their small star into the emptiness.

1955

GOTTFRIED BENN

Who Are You

Who are you – all the legends
are vanishing. What was –
chimeras, Leda's kindred
in genuflecting pass,

painted with blood of berries,
the scarlet drunkards, she –
the masculine-defying –
a fiery laurel tree,

with serpent hair the haunches,
by branch and thyrsus staff,
in drunken fit, finale,
and round a holy grave –

What is, are hollow corpses,
the rock and seawrack screen,
what seems, eternal token
that plays the whole depth clean –

in phantom fields, portrayal
inhabiting no form – :
Odysseus past affliction
who sleeping found his home.

1925

Duino Elegies, 5

dedicated to Frau Hertha Koenig

Who can they be, tell me, these wayfaring people, a little
more fleeting still than ourselves, wrung by a never
sated (yet for the sake of whom?) insistent will
from childhood on? But it wrings them,
bends them, loops them and hoists them,
hurls and catches them back; down they come
out of air as if it were oiled and smoother,
down on the tenuous carpet worn to the threads
by their perpetual upspring, this carpet
lost in the universe.
Applied like a dressing, as if the suburban
sky had hurt the earth.

       No sooner there,
erect, there, and shown: the great
initial of Thereness . . . , and the strongest of men,
it rolls them up, the always imminent grip,
for a joke, as Augustus the Strong at mealtime
a platter of tin.

Ah, and around this
centre the rose of onlooking – it comes
to flower, its petals fall. Around this
pestle, pistil, assailed by its own
flowering pollen, fertilized over again to become
the sham fruit of aversion, never
aware of itself, aversion smiling its faint
sham smile that shines with the thinnest of surfaces.

There, the flabby wrinkled lifter,
old man apt only for beating the drum,
sunk inside his enormous skin, as though once it contained
two men and one of them lay
in a churchyard already, the other surviving,
deaf and at times a little
vague in his widowed skin.

But the youngster, man, like the son of a neck
and a nun: packed to the brim
with muscle and simpleness.

O you people whom once
a sorrow acquired, when it was still
small, as a toy, in one of its
long convalescences . . .

You that fall with the thump
only fruits know, unripe, dropping each day
a hundred times from the tree of motion lofted
by common endeavour (swifter than water,
all in a moment it has spring and summer and autumn) –
fall and crash to the grave:
At times, in half of an interval, a tender face
wants to well up in you and float across to your seldom
kindly mother; but hardly attempted,
timid, the face is lost against
your body that flatly exhausts it . . . And again
the man is clapping his hands for the leap up, and
before any pain can take shape close to the ever
galloping heart, comes the tingle in the footsoles,
stealing a march on the source it springs from, with
a few physical tears chased into your eyes.
And yet, blindly,
the smile . . .

Angel, O take it, pluck it, the small-flowered herb that heals.
Shape a jar to preserve it. Place it among those joys
that are still not open to us; in some graceful urn
exalt it with an inscription, flowery, looping:
                                          'Subrisio saltat.'

You then, sweet one, mute
under the overleap
of joys bewitching. Perhaps
your frills are happy for you –
or crossing the young
firm breasts the green metallic silk
feels itself endlessly pampered and needs nothing.
You,

time and again in all the trembling balances placed
somewhat otherwise, market fruit of serenity,
public among the shoulders.

Where O where is the place – in my heart I hold it –
where to be *able* was still far off, and away from each other
they fell, like ill-matched
animals mounting each other; –
where weights are heavy still;
where from their sticks that twirl in vain
the dishes tumble . . .

And all of a sudden in this laborious Nowhere, all of a sudden
the unsayable place, where the pure Too Little
incomprehensibly changes – with a leap reversing
into that empty Too Much.
Where the multiple digits flash
to a sum beyond number.

Squares, O square in Paris, infinite scene
where Madame Lamort, the modiste,
entwines and loops the restless ways of the world,
ribbons unending, and from them invents
novelty bows, frills, flowers, cocades, artificial
fruits, all in false tints for the cheap
winter hats of Fate.
. . . .

Angel: supposing a place exists, unknown to us, and there
on a carpet that cannot be spoken of, lovers were showing,
lovers who cannot achieve it here, their
daring lofty figures of heart-leap,
towers of delight, their
ladders long since, where ground never was, leaning
atremble against one another, – suppose they achieved it,
ringed by spectators, the numberless hushed dead:
would then the dead throw down their last coins long saved,
hidden ones we know nothing of, their eternally
genuine coins of happiness to the pair
smiling in truth at last on the quietened
carpet?

1923 (written February 1922)

VELIMIR KHLEBNIKOV

(Khlebnikov's Kuznecik)

Quilleting his capillicules in a silverscript
Grasshopper piloted into his bellypot
Slips of osier,
Stipples, gobs of polypod.
Peen! Peen! marshtit boomdiyayed
Tara! Be swansome,
Shine, Phenomenamen!

1920 (?)

Horse Shaking Head

She saw in the field a horse, she put her arms around it.
The horse wanted to fly, it frisked in her embrace,
Flattened its ears, shook its head. 'Stop,' it said,
'I must go now.' Up to the clouds it slowly went,
Then it flew, flew at a gallop. It sees a city
Underneath, streets, factories, blocks of flats.
It doesn't stop, it flies over mountains, meadows,
But then, why, it sees a house, patched, and on a tilt,
Geraniums in tin cans at its windows,
Smoke rising from its chimney, out in front
Two poplars. Down to the roof it goes, hoofs
Hardly touch the tiles, and then it sleeps.
If a child belongs to the house and sees it,
She'll be thinking: There's a horse. She puts her arms around it.
The horse wants to fly, it frisks in her embrace,
Flattens its ears, shakes its head.

1980

LARS GUSTAFSSON

The Birds

Canal Landscape with Ten Locks,
in the Dutch Manner

In
under the trees, the old trees that loyally
shade the ancient canal
with its lock-keepers' whitewashed houses,
its beehives, vines, its friendly dogs,
too often asleep, black water,
where quick as a lightning flash the swallows fly
one inch above the surface, never faltering,
fly close to the flowing black water
which hides forever the lost coin
which, in turn, on its way to the bottom,
gliding, will perpetually give back
the golden brilliance of the original light.
Into the ancient canal systems
of a strange country that is forever
hidden between the highways,
where the ten old houses of lock-keepers
still carry inscriptions on their walls,
where toward evening the old taverns open
to travellers from all ten townships,
who manage to sit together more or less at peace,
the dogs fall asleep again in the verdure,
the swallows glide and the vapours lift
from the waters, homely, like slow thoughts,
here we can talk again, here the birds fly still,
here nobody troubles us and if somebody does
it's only because he's nobody.
And the coin gliding to the bottom
is forever on its way.

1984

HAROLDO DE CAMPOS

from *Galaxies*

passtimes and killtimes i wendaway darkling for mindamends through this minimeandering instant of minutes instancing somebody and instanced beyond to telltale a scheherazade thistory my fairy how many fates are there in each nullitywee thread discard nines leaving nought scheherazade scheherazade a nightstory a thousandtimes overtold then the sonnyboy soulumbering into this nightdark florest came and a drago sevensnouted dragoned his swellhand into a fernavid and cavernish grottohollow my boy wants knowhow to unpick this threadform how to sideslip this cavern only the dragon all dragoning knows the key to this festival and now the dragon at his siesta is asnoozing then when myboy began his ringawinnow round a rosaromanorum gesta in the bosk he stumbled on the sleepy beauty bellabella tell me a life thistory but sleepy beauty in the silence sleepeyed on and nobody told him if there was any forthgoes myboy to a kingdom interlunar where the dead king was up and the upwas king is dead but nobody told him the sideslip thistory myboy is only so posed now to suffer the firetrial to ford the bosk and florrage through the river for the headbone that is there in the well's depth in the depth of pickatomb and catafalque in this well is a caput mortuum myboy doth to godbye suffer a seachange in the caboose but the head does not tell the thistory of its well if there was or if there was not if it was girl or boy a swan of anothertime appears to him in a dream and to the swan country takes him swirling in a bird flock myboy asks the swan about the thistory he sings his swan song and swanenchants himself and now is Mrs Sun in the One-Who-Waits and her golden rain illuminates myboy she is in her danaë tower incubus princess crowned by a shower tell me your pluvial tale how it was the gold in a torrent of dust made spawn your treasure but auri-confused the princess of gold clammed up and for to find the taletale myboy wend on his way from post to pillar from muse to medusa all dot in white and white in dot scheherazade my fairy this is all going nowhere princess my princess what a thistory of maze-understanding how many more veins and volutes and volutions find me a verysimil that will make of speech the verity and transform in fate a fairy this sybilline simil of destiny's mercurianimal serpentine malefemale and in speech transforms the fate find me this wickedworking blindworm fish-word where the song sings the tale of the song where the why does not tell how where the egg searches in the egg for its retribrilliant ovality

where the fire became water the water a body of vapour where the
nude unmakes its not and the nut snows itself with nothing a fairy tells
a tale that is her deathsong but nobody not even a tiny one can know
of this fairy her tale where it begins indeed where it finishes there is no
soul to face for her to be told it she is all enchanted water go boy my
tinyboy to unimagine this fatamorgana is fatiguising a malefelonious
sentence you dig miles downunder and come out in the well where you
dig you work three hundred for three cent you change diamonds
myriads for a crude coal who knows if this coal might be the diamon-
diferous dust the mother-of-diamonds morgana of the charmstones
and the boy went and the legend does not tell of his ongoing if he came
back or did not if from his going one does not come back the legend
pokerface does not say only unsays only keeps going around and
around and around

published 1976 (1963–73)

KLABUND

Gentian

I

Sob, gentian blue!
The crags re-echo.
Water tastes iron,
heaven helmets my head.

The last snow weeps away
into moss.
Knees tremble here
in sharp descent.

Wind sings
in evenchill
and a child
behind houses.

II

If I knew why
I would know a little.
If I knew from where
I would know much.

The anchor on the sailor's arm
grasps flesh.
Your song floating from windows
is hushed.

That way the yacht sails,
the Rapid.
Salt lake breathes,
a white breast.

The huge seas! But no one saw
the tiny source in the alpine thicket.
Only a dying beaver
moistened its flews.

III

Days will come,
sunless without laughter.
Fields fallow.
No corn shines.

Corpses roll in the rivers,
trains are packed with mad passengers,
whoever has a heart weeps,
stooping over the cesspit.

Baldhead and blockhead
alternate like wild game.
The victory vanishes,
many carpets are worn thin.

A firtree
still stands – perhaps.
A chamois' horns hang
on the chasm's brink.

IV

An old mountain,
an old woman.
The hostel
is crumbling.

Ice and crags
are asleep.
Only a gust of wind
wakes.

Out of the valley the depths
rise glowing.
A bush of flowers burns now
on the slope.

Now bells waft over,
and a billygoat.
A little girl
smiles upward.

1917

HUGO BALL

The Sun

Through the slits of my eyes a perambulator passes.
Through the slits of my eyes walks a man with a poodle.
A treeclump turns into a cluster of snakes and hisses heavenward.
A stone makes a speech. Trees in Greenbrand. Escaping islands.
A swaying and a shell-tinkling and fish-head as on the floor of the ocean.

My legs stretch out right to the horizon. A carriage bangs
away over them. My boots soar on the horizon like the towers
of a sinking town. I am the Giant Goliath. I digest goat cheese.
I am a mammoth's calf. Green grassbugs snuffle me.
Grass spans green sabers and bridges and rainbows over my belly.

My ears are giant pink shells, open wide. My body swells
with the sounds that are trapped in it. I hear the bleating
of great Pan. I hear the vermilion music of the sun. It stands
up on the left. Its wisps flash vermilion into the world's night.
When it falls it will crush the town and the church towers
and all the front gardens full of crocus and hyacinth and will blare
like the tin of children's trumpets.

But in the air there is a counterblowing of crimson and egg-yellow
and bottle-green: swings that an orange fist holds on long threads,
and there is a singing from birdthroats that hop over branches.
A very fragile fencing of children's banners.

Tomorrow the sun will be loaded on a big-wheeled wagon
and taken to Caspari's art gallery. A beast-headed negro
with bulging neck, bladder nose and a long stride will hold fifty white
bucking asses like those yoked to wagons at the building of pyramids.

A crowd of bloodbright people will clot the street: midwives and
          wetnurses,
invalids in wheel chairs, a stilting crane, two female St Vitus dancers,
a man with a ribbed silk tie and a red-smelling policeman.

I can't stop myself: I'm full of joy. The window crossbars
shatter. A children's nurse hangs to her navel from a window.
I can't help myself: the cathedrals burst with organ-fugues. I want
to make a new sun. I want to strike two together
like cymbals, and to hold my hand to my lady. Away we shall float
in a violet sedan over the roofs of your
bright yellow town in the breeze like lampshades of tissue paper.

1914

ACHIM VON ARNIM

Little Humpback

In my garden onions grow,
I go to give them water,
Little Humpback, there he stands,
Starts to sneeze and sputter.

My kitchen when I go to it
To cook a soup with spices,
Little Humpback, there he stands,
He's broke my bowl in pieces.

I go into my dining room,
Hungry for apple cobbler,
Little Humpback, there he stands,
He's eaten half, the gobbler.

Into my cellar when I go
My barrel to be tapping,
Little Humpback, there he stands,
My wine jug now he's grabbing.

When for wood to make a fire
Into my shed I'm going,
Little Humpback, there he stands,
Half my store he's stolen.

I sit beside my spinning wheel,
Twist my thread for spinning,
Little Humpback, there he stands,
Stops my wheel from turning.

Into my bedroom when I go
To make my feather bed up,
Little Humpback, there he stands,
Starts to laugh his head off.

When I kneel to say a prayer,
Just as I begin it,
Little Humpback, there he stands,
Talks a mile a minute.

Ah, dear child, I ask of you:
Pray for Little Humpback too.

Early 1800s, from folk tradition

OSKAR LOERKE

from *The Stone Path*

A dream's my burden, leaden frost my foe;
The sky bows down its bare low brow again,
The white path coils and is a whorl of brain.
The world goes ignorant of where to go.

Over the world's unmoving course my way
The black Orc whistles, hunting seed, descends
And perches on the square of stone. He stands,
He pecks, then swallows, what, I cannot say.

Now fills the world his eyes' bird-flighted round.
His mind is set, all thought of mating fled.
In his beak's axe the cry of rut is dead.
In wrath diagonal he hacks the ground.

Into his eye the very rock seems gone;
The hardness grows, the glow of living wanes.
Only the beat of his horned axe remains
And, giving him no mercy now, the stone.

Like vices, and as merciless, the sheer
Blows batter down. They rob me of my mind
Till it awakens. And then outside I hear
The snow fall soft. A virgin glacier, with no wind
This warm and Christmas night, my path shines clear.

1938

6. THRESHOLDS

IBN ZAYDUN

From Al-Zahra

With passion from this place
    I remember you.
        Horizon clear, limpid

The face of earth, and wind,
    Come twilight, desists,
        A tenderness sweeps me

When I see the silver
    Coiling waterways
        Like necklaces detached

From throats. Delicious those
    Days we spent while fate
        Slept. There was peace, I mean,

And us, thieves of pleasure.
    Now only flowers
        With frost-bent stems I see;

At my eyes their vivid
    Centres pull, they gaze
        Back at me, seeing me

Without sleep, and a light
    Flickers through their cups,
        In sympathy, I think.

The sun-baked rose-buds in
    Bushes, remember
        How their colour had lit

Our morning air; and still
    Breaths of wind dispense
        At break of day, as then,

Perfume they gather up
    From waterlilies'
        Half-open drowsy eyes.

Such fresh memories
    Of you these few things
        Waken in my mind. For

Faraway as you are
    In this passion's grip
        I persist with a sigh

And pine to be at one
    With you. Please God no
        Calm or oblivion

Will occupy my heart,
    Or close it. Listen
        To the shiver of wings

At your side – it is my
    Desire, and still, still
        I am shaking with it [. . .]

Pure love we once exchanged,
    It was an unfenced
        Field and we ran there, free

Like horses. But alone
    I now can lay claim
        To have kept faith. You left,

Left this place. In sorrow
    To be here again,
        I am loving you.

11th century

GEORG TRAKL

Western Song

O the soul's nocturnal wingbeat:
Shepherds we walked by dusky forests once
And the red deer followed, the green flower and babbling stream,
Humbly. O the ancient sound of the little cricket,
Blood flowering on the sacrificial slab
And the lonely birdcry over the pond's green calm.

O you crusades and glowing tortures
Of the flesh, descent of the crimson fruits
In the garden at evening where long ago the pious disciples walked,
People now of war, from wounds and star-dreams waking.
O the gentle cornflower sheaf of night.

O you times of quietness and golden autumns
When peaceful monks we trod the purple grape;
And hill and forest shone around us.
O you hunts and castles; peace at evening,
When in his room man meditated justice,
Wrestled in dumb prayer for the living head of God.

O the bitter hour of decline,
When we regard a stony face in black waters.
But radiant the lovers raise their silver eyelids:
One kin. From rosy pillows incense pours
And the sweet canticle of the bodies resurrected.

1914

FRIEDRICH HÖLDERLIN

The Ages of Life

You cities of Euphrates!
Narrow streets of Palmyra!
Forests of columns in the desert plain,
What are you?
Fume of gods and
Fire stript off
Your crowns as you crossed
The boundary of breath;
But now I sit under clouds (each
With its own repose), under
Sumptuous oaks, on
The roebuck's heath, and alien
They seem to me, dead,
The blessèd souls.

1803 (?)

EDUARD MÖRIKE

The Beautiful Beech Tree

Hidden deep in the wood I know of a place where a beech tree
  Stands, in beauty beyond any a picture can show.
Clean and smooth it rises up, strong-bodied, aloof,
  Swathed in silken allure none of its neighbours can touch.
Round it, far as the noble tree puts branches forth,
  Grows, delighting the eye, turf in a ring of green;
With radius always constant it circles the trunk in the centre,
  Artlessly nature herself shaped this charming surround.
First it is fringed by wispy bushes; further back
  Trees with towering boles fend the heavenly blue.
Fulsome the dark oak grows and beside it the virginal
  Crest of the birch that, shy, sways in the golden light.
Only the spot where the path disappears, half-hidden by rocks,
  Out of the glade gives a hint of open country beyond.
– Not long since, walking alone, as the summery shapes,
  New, had lured me away from the path and I lost myself
In the bushes, a friendly spirit, the listening god of the grove,
  Led me here for the first time and in wonder I stood.
What delight! It was the moment of high noon,
  Everything was hushed, even the birds in the leaves.
And I was hesitant still to tread on the exquisite carpet;
  A ceremony it seemed, at length as I stole across.
Then, as I leaned against the trunk (its canopy billows
  Out not much overhead), freely my widening gaze
Followed the burning ray of the sun as it ran in a circle,
  Edging the shadowy round, almost measuring it.
There I stood, without moving, listening deep in myself
  To the demonic stillness, calm unfathomable.
With you enclosed in this magic circle of sun my only
  Thought, O solitude, my only feeling was you.

1838

The Convent at Fahr

Still flowering garden of the past, calm suburb of heaven
In wisps of cloud, and poplars, wheat hills, and shining water,
Through vegetable plots the nuns meander, summer wind
Plays in their robes'
Indolent flags, and the fragrance
Of white carnations
Surges across with a warm breath of chicken yard.

Coyly they close
Their doors on the sweet world, gather themselves
Into God's depth, heavenly vaticans
Dazzle the soul which eagerly,
And by long patience fatigued,
Consumes itself
In the calm of scrutiny –
O infinitely
Beyond words the windows glitter!

More than all else they love
Their grave
In the burial ground, in shadowy shale, there they will crumble
Where the rain-gutted
Sanctum of a church, with an Apocalypse
Upon the walls and moss-cold angel
Clouds amid ivy, every flame extinct, contains
Their eternity's severe repose.

Quietly yet the fish now darken
Through bushy alder, harvests gush, in farmers' cradles
Thrives generation on generation
Of rugged countrymen, the horses stamp, the byres
Are redolent with streams of holy milk
When lanterns at daybreak
With a blue radiance
Gleam in the haylofts.
Golden straws
That litter the road
Sparkle and shift like summer lightning.

But wearily from dun sage
And phlox in clusters
The petals flake into candles
Encircling the feet
Of the saints.
God's prisoners
Waver in cells, while far off
With black spikes and silos,
Gasometers and cathedrals, the sunset town
Bathed in its hellish crimson
Is darkening under the hills.

1936

IBN SARA

A Pool with Turtles

Eyelashes thick
And a pupil
Among flowers
The secluded pool
How beautiful

With turtles in it
How they leap
In fun and pop up
Clad
Moss green

Squabble
For places at
The pool's rim
But come winter
Plunge deep

Down and all
Stay hidden
At any time
When they are playing
Watch them flip

And peer around
For all the world
Like Christian
Soldiers with
Shouldered shields

c. 1100

EDUARD MÖRIKE

In a Park

Look how they hang, the childish leaves of the chestnut, still
  Moist like butterfly wings fresh from the broken cocoon;
But nights are warm and the briefest sprinkle of rain descending
  Quietly spreads their fans, roofing the alley of air.
Whether you hurry or stay, heavenly spring, always you sweep
  Over the drunken mind, soon like a miracle gone.

1847

FRIEDRICH HÖLDERLIN

Like Sea Coasts . . .

Like sea coasts when the gods begin to build
  and
    rushing splendour the wave creations
  hove inshore
      and earth
        robes in her panoplies
soon
    with one
    joymost in good mood and hoarding it
    so
bearing the winegod
      for his importance much
    being promised
also of Greece the darling
        born of the sea
        her gaze modest
beats the tremendous
    billowing treasure
      up shores of song.

1803–4 (?)

AL-MU'TAMID

To Abu Bakr Ibn 'Ammar Going to Silves

When you come to Silves, Abu Bakr, my friend,
Greet with my burning love the spirits who dwell
In that place, and ask if any remember me.
Say this young man still sighs for the white palace,
The Alcazar of Lattices, where men like lions,
Warriors live, as in a wild beast's den,
And in soft boudoirs women who are beautiful.
Sheltered under the wing of darkness,
How many nights I spent with girls there.
Slender at the waist, hips round and abundant,
Tawny hair or golden, deeper than a sword blade
Or black lance their charms would run me through.
How many nights, too, in the river's loop I spent
With a graceful slave girl for my companion;
The curve of her bracelet imitated the river.
She poured out for me the wine of her eyes;
Or again the wine of her nook she poured for me;
Another time it was the wine of her lips she poured.
When her white fingers played among lute strings,
I felt a thrill as when a sword hits and clips
Clean through the sinews of a foe in combat.
When with a languid look she'd shake off her robe,
Like a ray of light surrendering her body was.
The very air around her shivered with desire.
It was a rose opening out of a rosebud.

c. 1065

TRISTAN TZARA

Maison Flake

Unleash bugles   the announcement vast and glassy   animals of the
                                                         maritime agency
aerostatic forester   all that exists strides at a gallop   of clarity life
the angel has white lips   umbrella   virility
snow licks the road   and the lily verified virgin
3/25 in altitude   a new meridian passes this way
stretched bow of my heart   typewriter to write for the stars
who told you 'chopped foam of prodigious sorrows-   clock'
offers you a word one does not find in Larousse
and wants to reach your height

what steam of a tube of lightning pushes
ours against the eternal multiform veil
here one does not assassinate people on the terraces
which colour themselves from the intimate sequence of slownesses

we are attempting unheard-of things
mirages in quarto   micrographies of chromatic souls and of images
we all carry the jinglebell tumult which we shake
for the major festivals on the viaducts and for the animals

turn of a dance   in octavo   on meteor and violin
the play of ices   year that passes
let's have a drink   I'm a crazy person
ink of sky   lake of honeywater
opaque wine   Flake in a hammock

practice   the quiet and fecund offering
he scrapes the sky with his fingernails
and the skyscraper is only his shadow
in a bathrobe

the year will be   among the palm and banana trees   spurted from the
                                                          halo in cubes of water
simple productive vast music   surging safe into port
and the crimson bread in the future and multiple season
some old etchings of kings out hunting prettily coloured

pipe and boxing   in the vase   beneath the ace of spades   piddler with
the birds and fallow nudes   a vigilant boat in their beak
of rock   motor with sparks   good news   the Eiffel Tower is playing
the rebeck
here every chair is soft and comfortable like an archbishop
ascetic enterprise   monks guaranteed   at all prices   ladies, here it is
Maison Flake

1917 (?)

Text spaced out in order to indicate ruptures and collisions. Otto Flake (pro-
nounced *Flahkeh*) was a German novelist sympathetic to the young Dada poets
and artists in Zürich, 1916–19 (see his *roman à clef, Nein und Ja*). Tristan Tzara
was the name adopted by Semi Rosenstock from Romania (1896–1963). He
was one of the original members of Hugo Ball's group at the Holländische
Meierei, later called Cabaret Voltaire. The French original, which is a maze of
assonance and alliteration, ending with an insistent rhyme on *-ec*, has been
spaced out in translation to accentuate the disjunctions that Tzara probably
modelled, with absurd magnifications, on Marinetti's Italian Futurist texts, and
possibly on Apollinaire's *Calligrammes*. With Tzara's move to Paris (end of
1919), disjunction invaded Paris Dada and Surrealist poems, to pass eventual-
ly into the 'New York School' poetics of the 1960s, e.g. Frank O'Hara, John
Ashbery, John Wieners, *et al.*

171

IBN KHAFAJA

The River

God how beautiful it was
Gliding in its bed, the river

To drink from, more delicious
Than a lovely woman's lips

The loops, bracelets
Everywhere flowers ringed it

Milky Way

Margins of boughs curled like
Eyelashes, clear river iris

A breeze, later afternoon
Teased the boughs
Gold of dusk skimming
Silver water

c. 1100

FRIEDRICH HÖLDERLIN

Greece
Third version

O you voices of fate, you
              Pathways of man
                   Travelling!
  For the unruffled mood
Of clouds, like blackbird song, sounds
     From afar in the blueness
    Of the school, in the rushing
          Of the sky, tuned
To harmony by storm that is
        God's being-there.

   And shouts, like
        Lookings-out toward
Immortality and heroes;
         Manifold
  Memories are, to which a vibrance
Clings, of earth, as to a drumskin, from
     Destructions,
         Temptations of saints,
   For the work shapes itself
In the beginning, obeys
       Great laws, and afterward
Choral
   Clouds appear, singing
         Knowledge, tenderness, the sweep
Of sky – all
    Integument.

For fixed and firm is
The earth navel. Shores of grass
            Batten down
                  The flames and universal
Elements. But pure
            And utter consciousness
                        Aither lives above. The light
Yet
      On clear days is
                  Silver. Signifying love,
Earth is violet.

            Grand beginnings, too,
Can come to little. But day in, day out,
                  God wears a garment
Wonderfully for the favour of man.
                        And his face hides
      From cognizance, and robes
                  The air with art.
And air and time
            Robe God the Terrifier, lest
One thing love him
            Overmuch, or the soul do. For nature
      Was always news, an open book
To learn from, or lines
                  And angles, yellower the suns,
                        Yellower the moons,

But times do come
When the old shaping imageries
              Of earth launch forth –
      In histories,
                  Happenings past, brave
              Battlings, when God
Leads earth from height
      To height. But he sets
                  A limit to the stride unchecked
By measure, then
      The soul's powers and
      Affinities draw in tight,
              As golden blossoms do, together,
  So that beauty may dwell on earth
More fondly, and a spirit of some kind
      Makes commoner cause with men.

      Sweet then it is to dwell
Sunnily in the tall
      Shade of tree and hill, where
              There is a paved path goes to the church.
But for travellers, with whom
      The feet comply, moving in measure, on and on
For love of life,
              The pathways flower, lovelier yet,
      Where the countryside

1803–4 (?) – unfinished

175

LARS GUSTAFSSON

Ballad of the Paths in Västmanland

Under the visible script of small tracks,
gravel tracks, forest tracks, often with a grass
ridge in the middle, between deep ruts
hidden beneath twigs heaped in clearings,
still distinct in crumbling moss,
another script runs: the old paths.
They lead from lake to lake, from valley
to valley. Sometimes deeper furrows,
more distinct, and sturdy bridges
of medieval stone carry them over black streams;
sometimes they evaporate on bare rocky ground;
you lose them easily in swamps, so
imperceptibly that one moment they are there,
and the next not. They do go on,
always there's a going on, you only have
to seek, the paths are obstinate,
they know what they want, and with that knowledge
they combine considerable cunning.
You walk east, the compass points insistently east,
faithfully the path follows the compass, like a streak,
all is well, then the path veers north.
And north there's nothing. What does the path want?
Soon comes an enormous moor, and the path knew it.
It leads us around, with the certainty of someone
who knows what's what. It knows where the moor is;
it knows where the hill is too steep; it knows
what happens to someone who circles the lake
to the north instead of south. It has done it all,
so many times, before. That's the whole
point of being a path: it came to be made
long ago. Who made it? Charcoal burners, fisherfolk,
women with skinny arms, gathering firewood?
The outlaws, shysters, grey as the moss,
still in their dreams the blood of fratricide
reddens their hands. Autumn hunters on the tracks
of pointer dogs with barks clear as frost?
All of them, none of them. We make the path together,

you too, on a stormy day, on earth,
be the hour late or early:
we write the paths and they stick,
and the paths are more clever than us,
and they know all the things we wanted to know.

1980

IBN ABI RUH

Honey River

Next time you're passing Honey River stop
And ask about the night I spent there once
Till break of day confounding the police
And drinking wine from mouth to mouth it flowed
And cutting roses (as we say)

As branches interlace across a stream
So we embraced and drank fresh cups of wine
Our intertwining limbs ask too of them
And what it meant the cool word *aquilon*
Upon that flowery river bank

Where neither fire burned nor brazier stood
Yet what aromas all the flowers dispensed
Of aloë and ask about the candle flames
Aflicker in the river like the tips of swords
For so we loved without

Pause through the honey night until the cold
Necklaces we wore drove us at last apart
And all
I knew of melancholy or would ever know
Called in the last dawn song of a nightingale

12th century

178

JOHANN WOLFGANG VON GOETHE

A Winter Journey in the Harz

As the buzzard aloft
On heavy daybreak cloud
With easy pinion rests
Searching for prey,
May my song hover.

    For a god has
Duly to each
His path prefixed,
And the fortunate man
Runs fast and joyfully
To his journey's end;
But he whose heart
Misfortune constricted
Struggles in vain
To break from the bonds
Of the brazen thread
Which the shears, so bitter still,
Cut once alone.

    Into grisly thickets
The rough beasts run,
And with the sparrows
The rich long since have
Sunk in their swamps.

    Easy it is to follow that car
Which Fortune steers,
Like the leisurely troop that rides
The fine highroads
Behind the array of the Prince.

    But who is it stands aloof?
His path is lost in the brake,
Behind him the shrubs
Close and he's gone,
Grass grows straight again,
The emptiness swallows him.

O who shall heal his agony then
In whom each balm turned poison,
Who drank hatred of man
From the very fullness of love?
First held now holding in contempt,
In secret he consumes
His own particular good
In selfhood unsated.

If on your psaltery,
Father of love, there sounds
One note his ear can hear,
Refresh with it then his heart!
Open his clouded gaze
To the thousand fountainheads
About him as he thirsts
In the desert!

You who give joys that are manifold,
To each his overflowing share,
Bless the companions that hunt
On the spoor of the beasts
With young exuberance
Of glad desire to kill,
Tardy avengers of outrage
For so long repelled in vain
By the cudgelling countryman.

But hide the solitary man
In your sheer gold cloud!
Till roses flower again
Surround with winter-green
The moistened hair,
O love, of your poet!

With your lantern glowing
You light his way
Over the fords by night,
On impassable tracks
Through the void countryside;
With daybreak thousand-hued
Into his heart you laugh;

With the mordant storm
You bear him aloft;
Winter streams plunge from the crag
Into his songs,
And his altar of sweetest thanks
Is the snow-hung brow
Of the terrible peak
People in their imaginings crowned
With spirit dances.

You stand with heart unplumbed
Mysteriously revealed
Above the marvelling world
And you look from clouds
On the kingdoms and magnificence
Which from your brothers' veins beside you
With streams you water.

1777

EDUARD MÖRIKE

Afternoon

(from *Pictures from Bebenhausen*)

Three o'clock strikes in the abbey. How clear the trembling sound
    Slides through the breathless hush down to the edge of the wood,
Where it trickles away and sweetly melts into the hum of bees
    Surrounding me here as I sit quietly under the pines.

1867 (written September 1863)

A Desert with High Heels

entities and looking beyond them – lenses
I pupil them – they pupil too

as for statistics of pores and hair
like scalp over cobra – to shrinkhead

then what is a country so apprehended
in relation to the medium small town

lobes and spores of expellees
displaced into a kind of passage – desert

dunno are they well fed and on the stretch
people one meets are never missing legs

their foot region seems bashful to me
yet treading itself is unabashed

undeservedly static – mountain and valley appear
nothing but longtimes there – simply their golgotha

truly exotic in them – my similarity
from time to time expulsed from their illusion

specifically there'd be then a tuftytuft
the sort to be found three houses further on

at certain spots ventilation becomes a point
but now that's what dustdevil screws are for

whoever's childhood they realized / realize
this country is for me The Catcher in the Rye's

1986

GÜNTER KUNERT

Berlin Afternoon

In summer under a cloudy sky
in summer with a mild rain falling
in summer in the coolness of old rooms
in among old wallpapers freighted with visions:
to lie there
and listen to the trams
clunk of wheels over gaps in the rails
gallop of cabs
staccato of hand-driven machines
in blown-away back yards
mortal play of vanished bodies
pale in the pallor of secret beds
hidden behind crumbling stucco
behind the teeming scurf of old houses
which one sudden afternoon unwreathed
are carried away by dump trucks and cranes
complete with their contents
out of their existence into our memory
where their transience welcomed and wept for
stops: in summer
with a mild rain falling.

1968

OKTAY RIFAT

A Cloud for a Sailing Ship

Swallows come for the cloud
and stay above my rooftop,
no rain, the backyard walnut
wants to be seen from underneath its branches,
going red so it can be seen
it invites the swallows,
rain wants to cling to the windowpane,
and like the fishwife's earrings
daylight still remaining in the day
wants widows, girls, brides, babies,
evening comes, want it or not,
moonrise,
and the sailing ship like sugar candy
takes the moon from the sky, escorting
from tooth to tooth
its scent of a carnation.

1984

ROBERT WALSER

A Woman's Awe-Inspiring Blouse

A woman's awe-inspiring blouse
is hanging on a wall inside a house.
What splendid lines to start some poetry.
Might any other thoughts occur to me?
On the porch that I am looking over
(with eyes in which one should be a believer,
while busily building up on what they scan)
sits a skyblue painted water can –
behind an opulent umbrella, fruit
of an established firm of old repute –
in an invisible bathtub, what is more,
a girl, at this beguiling early hour,
tones up her measured rounds with nothing wetter
than fondling wet; a table next, a letter,
a tiny little letter on it, trifles
away, encircled sweetly by its riffles
and decorative garlands, thus, the time
I shorten with a pleasure quite sublime
by turning versicles that chance to rhyme.
Astonishingly prosaic they may sound, but I'm
quite unaware of any obligation else.
Can that be beef marinade this poet smells?
It conjures up a hungriness in me.
Meanwhile I find it unbelievably
beautiful how softly now the thin
branches move to whispers of the wind's violin,
and falling silent also, now I will
in rapture lean across the windowsill.

Mid 1920s

OSKAR PASTIOR

Filling Station

The Farmer takes the Poet into the grave with him, the
Poet takes the Knight into the grave with him; Castle,
Sensor, and Scene Change are likewise Trophies, which
the Castle, the Sensor, and the Scene Change take into
the Operyhouse – the overture astounds posterity: in

the stovepipe an exchange of words ignites; until the
door swings the other way open; the Barman takes the
Bottle from the Shelf; generally movie theatres take
Old Strangers into the grave with them – they are, to
be sure, Rooms and not Distancings; their sense for
Noses hanging from the Flies is more stunted than their
sense for Old Archives; the Farmer takes the Poet to

San Francisco with him, where they exchange Trophies
together – first aid for Bishops, Sensors, and Scene
Change; here I have nothing particular in mind; the
giving of Names never was the Question; the Road takes
the Opera on its Shoulders and trundles home with it;
the operetta sleeps the Old Gold Rush off.

1986

GÜNTER KUNERT

Zoo

Relatives with Latin names
faces of hide and plume
hands of leather and horn
eyes like glass
you can see through
to the depth of evolution
where the simple feelings live
fear and longing
old and sombre shadows

Your gaze
comes back from there
changed by the journey
strange
it looks at you as if
you had no part in it now

1980

OKTAY RIFAT

Like All Houses

Roads in the cup of a hand –
I see the bastions there,
you walk along the corridors
of incomprehensible sleep,
arrive in the serpent house,
the first haunted attic,
the first bed where we made love.

1984

ANDREAS OKOPENKO

Green Melody

> . . . *green melody blue girl*
> *holidays are white.*

I green in the meadow of the young village
My farm is yellow with girl with grain
My girl is yellow with farm with grain
I green in the grain of the young village

The sun is on the way to market
My girl is on the way to market
My green grain girl my green meadow girl
My green young village girl is on the way to market

The marketplaces are with pumpkins
The pumpkins are white dust of the marketplaces
The white dust of the noonday marketplaces
The white dust the way to the house to the girl to the garden

I green the afternoon in the girl garden
I am greening in the girl garden now
A cool room a blue check cloth
A noonday jug a blue glass a water

A younger sister intently playing the children's green
A younger sister who goes away and leaves us alone
The children's game the water splashes blue
My girl in the cool room apart

I am the cool room I am in the cool room
I am where at last the girl is I am with the girl
The girl and the water I drink the water
The jug is the room it takes us both

An ant crawls across the Latin grammar
A leaf has come in through the window
A drop of water has run across my mouth
A slow small clock makes the afternoon of aluminium

I shine silver in the sun like aluminium
I have buried my clock in earth in the flowerpot
My girl is not the beetle that runs across the wood
My girl lies in her summer dress on the window sill

On the window sill on the slight chair on the light cupboard
On the shadow the memory of sun on the afternoon the garden
I well understand the little boy that goes to play cards
I understand the little girl that keeps her fingers in green leaves

I know that Pythagoras is important and Aristides and Caesar
I am in revolt against the hidebound school
The blackboard the rule the school physician the chalk being dry
The duster being damp the sandwich paper being brown

I please the holidays of the children the little ones the beetles
The water the blue mirror the sunburn the railway
The farmdog the yellow one, the little pups the furballs
The red bow of the cat, the mouse in the trap with the bacon

I am the holidays I am the green
I green on the meadow in the grain
I blue in the room of the girl
In the afternoon, I blue in the girl.

1959

GÜNTER EICH

Ryoanji

Smoke signals for friends,
the day propitious, no wind,
to northeast, on the slope,
there's an answer for me, white.
I mix pine into it, and jawbone.
And now wall to wall
with theories of language,
wall to wall
my misery coughs with gold teeth,
on the walkways of wood
rain and wooden sandals,
I'm coming everywhere to an end,
my careworn toes
move in the dark
the darkness,
I regret myself,
I don't agree with my toes,
don't agree with my regret,
I miss the smoke signals,
old, black, and affectionate.
Now they no longer come,
now it is night,
now comes the fire,
all being for the best,
all for the worst.

I think nothing of the fire,
I think nothing of the smoke
and nothing of my breath.
I think something of coughing,
of sputum,
of the dark ideas of sickness,
of the darkness.
Cameras too are foreign to me,
so are the pine trees in flower pots.
I understand the kaki fruit better
and howling Old Japanese,

bowings at the end of the escalator,
and raw fish.

And many words with and,
and all of them
treacherously heartrending,
heart, hallo,
hallo to the renders,
perhaps there'd be
paper boats on the Kamo,
folded petitions,

that would be it,
entrusted to the uninfluential
oft-sung puddle
they anchor and wait
for the petitioners to collapse
and concluding remarks.

Temperatures rise
evenings in the clinic beds,
you learn things there,
the proofs for some of them
are not valid,
wilted leaves rustle
in the waste paper basket,
the hedgehogs under bushes,
almost dumb,
live responsive
to the prickly hide of my insights,
we rub them against one another,
at most moss is moved,
the world is not.
We exchange addresses,
we exchange our
personal recommendations,

we have much in common,
the risings of the sun,
the future up to nineteen seven.
Then we do breathing exercises,
together,

according to the rules of Cheyne
and the rules of Stokes,
so we pass the time away lightly
with the snoring nasals
of our most intimate thoughts.

Anyone wanting to,
let him hang photos in the display cases,
tell anecdotes
or listen to some,
discuss the situation,
ornithology, calligraphy,
Good Night above all.
We persist, a resolute clan,
with our hedgehogs
at the crucial moment,
for us there's no turning back now
to where, in baskets, sacks, tubs
past event piles up,

a storehouse, open to anyone,
doors slam, footsteps ring,
we don't hearken, we're deaf, too,
our dwelling is in free fall.
Bushes, darknesses and clinic beds,
now we never settle down,
we teach our daughters and our sons
the hedgehog words
and we abide by misrule,
the world does not work out
for friends of ours.

1966

GÜNTER KUNERT

Film Put in Backwards

When I woke
I woke in the breathless black
Of the box.
        I heard: the earth
Was opening over me. Clods
Fluttered back
        To the shovel. The
Dear box, with me the dear
        Departed, gently rose.
The lid flew up and I
Stood, feeling:
        Three bullets travel
Out of my chest
Into the rifles of soldiers, who
        Marched off, gasping
Out of the air a song
With calm firm steps
        Backwards.

1965

7. FIRST AND LAST THINGS

Testament

Ladies of virtue, honourable men,
   I ask of you, oblige me now:
You welcome me with love, so show
   Respect more deep than you have done.
Gratitude now you have larger cause to prove.
   Ask me why and I will tell you it:
These forty years I have sung and sing of love,
   The way it goes, its manners among men.
      Once like others I was glad of it,
      Now take no joy, while you play on;
      I serve you still with my love song,
      Honour the only gain I had of it.

So let my toil not yet be done,
   So let me go with a beggar's staff
And seek out virtue, as I have
   Sought far and wide, from boyhood on.
Then shall I be, humble perhaps, yet so
   Upstanding as any noble man:
Vexation for the pauper heart, although
   Men of virtue honour me the more.
      That we may foster them with praise,
      Virtues must be perpetual.
      A man esteems life not at all,
      Aspire he not to their embrace.

World, I have known your paying off:
   What once you gave, you took again.
Naked we leave you, every one.
   Shame on you if that's how I must leave.
Body and soul, too much, a thousand times
   I gambled upon your game away;
Old as I am, still fooled by tricks you play,
   If I am bitter, you deride me still.
      Laugh now, if laugh you must:
      Your day of grief will break anon,
      Your swag be stolen, flame burn:
      All comes tumbling down to dust.

Image I had of beauty then:
  Alas, I looked her in the face,
Sweetly conversing knew her ways:
  Now are the voices, now the beauty gone.
In her was wonder, gone whither I know not,
  And into silence gone the images.
Oh, and the lily rose is a prison gate
    For it has lost all colour, all perfume.
        Image of mine, if still your chain
        Binds me, let me now go free:
        Thus, to keep you company
        I'd go behind the bars again.

May then my soul survive decease.
  To many a heart have I brought down
Gladness, for woman and for man:
  Had I but known my own to please.
Yet when I praise bodily love, the soul mourns,
  Saying it is a lie, and I a fool:
Tells of the faith which true love owns:
    It lasts for ever, being virtual.
        Body, quit now the love that's gone,
        Honour the perpetuity of love:
        The very thing you sought does prove
        To be nor fish nor a fish bone.

c. 1227–30

The virgin, blithe and beautiful today

The virgin, blithe and beautiful today
Will it for us with drunken wingbeat break
This lid of ice, this hard forgotten lake
A glacier haunts, of flights not flown away

A Swan of other time remembers it is he,
Magnificent but hopeless, has to yield,
Having not sung for life more far afield
When sterile winter gleamed with its ennui

All his neck will shake this agony of white
Which space inflicts on the bird denying it
But not earth's horror gripping every plume

Phantom, hither by his pure splendour drawn,
Slow he settles in the cold disdainful dream
Which in his vacant exile cloaks the Swan

1885

IBN KHAFAJA

The Mountain Poem

By your life, there is no telling
    If the wind's bluster or camel's back
Put the speed under my saddle

For no sooner, dawn star, do I
    Soar up in the east to be born
Than I have cruised west at day's end

Alone, by one desert delivered
    To the next and seeing through
Night's mask the manifold face of death

No friend but my pointy sword
    No home but the saddle
I meet with nobody

No company is mine at all
    But the ghost of a smile
A hope intermittent in desire

And night everlasting proves
    False the dawn,
False the foretelling of it

Black dreadlocks of night eternal
    Trail behind me
Always I hug such bright hopes

Yet night's shirt I did once rip
    And saw beneath
Fangs agape, a grey wolf

A dark one, grey as dawn
    And peering out like stars
For so his eyes were burning

Then I came to a mountain
      Reaching up and up
Its peak achieved the meridian

It blocked every which way
      The rushing winds and at night
It shouldered the stars

Arched over the desert a mountain
      Like some thinker
Weighing all the consequences

Clouds like turbans, black, wrap him
      Lightning fringed them
With tufts of crimson

And mute as he was, languageless,
      On my night journey I heard him
Speak to me of the mysteries:

To the murderers, he told me,
      I gave refuge, to men grieving
And patient ascetics a shelter

How many nights when, coming, or going
      A traveller passed me by
How many caravans in my shadow rested

How often the wild winds
      Whacked my flanks and emerald
Oceans crowded me in

Yet did death's hand take all, folded
      Every one away, in a wink
The killjoy winds blew them off

My trees will stir – only the shudder
      Of human ribs; and my doves,
When they call it is a keening

What stopped my tears was not
      Forgetting, but an exhaustion
I had wept them all out with farewells

How long will I be in this place
      While friends move on, how often
See the backs of all who do not return?

Till what time must I contemplate
      Stars that rise and set
Forever and ever and on?

Have mercy, Lord, a mountain asks you
      Hear his prayer, touch with your Grace
The hand, uplifted, of your lover

Such was the sermon I heard
      One might learn less of matters
In the compass of a lifetime

In tears he stirred, grief excited
      Such consolation was mine
He was the best friend to travel with

As the track veered away, me with it,
      I answered him: Peace,
One of us has to stay and one move on.

c. 1100

RAINER MARIA RILKE

Duino Elegies, 10

That I may sing anon, coming out of the grim insight,
exultation and praise to an amen from angels.
That of the heart's hammers, clearly striking,
none may falter on slack or hesitant or
brittle strings. That my streaming face may make me
more radiant; that the mute weeping
may blossom. How I will cherish you then,
tormented nights. Unconsolable sisters, more humbly still,
kneeling, I should have welcomed you, let myself go
more loosely into your loosened hair. Us – we are wasters of pain.
How we foresee it, down the long sad view, and think
perhaps it will end. Yet surely pain is a foliage
lasts through winter, our musing's dark green,
one season of the secret year – not only season,
but place, estate, store, homestead, dwelling.

And still how strange are the alleys of Misery Ville,
where in the false hush contrived of deafening clamour,
out of vacuity's mold the bluster
gushes: the gilded uproar, bloated memorial.
Oh, how the tread of an angel would crush their Comfort Market,
boundaried by the church they bought readymade,
tidy and locked and forlorn as a Post Office on Sunday.
But outside, always there, the curly fringe of the Fairground.
Swings of Freedom! Tumblers and Jugglers of Zeal!
And the figured shooting stand of Fortune prettified,
seething with targets, where tin rings hollow
if a smarter marksman hits. From applause to potluck
on he spins, a booth for every curious craving
woos and drums and bellows. Yet for adults
especially to be seen – the way money multiplies, anatomic, not
entertainment only: money's genitals,
all, the works, the process – that's the lesson
makes you fertile ………
……………Oh, but just beyond, behind
the last hoarding where 'Deathless', that bitter beer,
is advertised, which seems to the drinkers sweet

as long as fresh distraction is there to nibble on . . .
just at the back of the hoarding, behind it, *reality* occurs.
Children are playing, lovers hold each other, – separate,
serious, in the scant grass, and dogs respond to nature.
The young man, on he's drawn, further still, perhaps he likes
a young Lament . . . He's after her, into the fields. She says:
– Far. We live out there . . .
                              Where? and the young man
follows her. Touched by her bearing. Shoulders, throat, perhaps
a noble lineage? Yet he is quitting her, turns back,
turns, and waves . . . Why trouble? She's a Lament.

Only the young dead in the first condition
of timeless composure, weaned from habit,
follow her lovingly. Girls,
she waits for them, making friends. Shows them quietly
what she is wearing. Pearls of Sorrow, and her delicate
Veils of Endurance. – With young men she walks in silence.

But there, where they live, in the valley, one of the older
Lament girls
takes care of the young man when he questions her: 'We were,'
she says, 'once a Great Family, we Laments. Our fathers
mined over yonder the big mountains; among people
sometimes you find a fragment of primal sorrow, burnished, sharp,
or from an old volcano slaggily petrified rage.
Yes, it comes from there. Once we were rich.'

And lightly she guides him through the open Lament country,
shows him the temple columns, or the ruins
of those strongholds where the Prince Laments of the foretime
wisely governed the land. Shows him the tall
Trees of Tears, and Fields of Sadness in Flower
(known to the living only as tender leaves);
shows him at pasture the Beasts of Grief, – and sometimes
a bird takes fright and pens as it skims through their up-gaze
extensively the script of its desolate cry. –
At sundown she takes him to the ancestral tombs,
every one a Lament, the Sibyls and Lords of Warning.
But as night comes close, they walk more softly and soon
the tombstone moon that watches over All
starts to rise. Brother to that tomb on the Nile,

sublime, the Sphinx: the countenance
of hushed interior chambers.
And they wonder at the crownlike head, which, for ever,
mutely, put the human face
in the balance of the stars.

His look cannot encompass it, dizzy
in early death. But her gaze
scares from behind the brim of the pschent an owl. And it
with a slow downstroke touching his cheek,
the one with the ripest rondure,
softly traces in the new
death-hearing, across a double
opened page, the indescribable outline.

And higher, the stars. New ones. The stars of Sorrow Land.
Slowly the Lament names them: Here,
look: the Horseman, the Wand, and the fuller constellation
they call the Fruit Garland. Then, further, toward the Polestar:
Cradle; Path; The Burning Book; Puppet; Window.
But in the southern sky, pure as in the palm
of a sainted hand, the clear and radiant M,
which means Mothers . . .

Yet the dead must plod on; in silence the older Lament girl
brings him to the Ravine
where there's a shimmer in the moonlight:
the Spring of Joy. In awe
she names it, says: Among people it is
a sustaining stream.

They stop at the foot of the mountains.
And there she embraces him, weeping.

Alone he starts to ascend the mountain of Primal Sorrow.
Even his footsteps make no sound where Fate allows none.

But the infinitely dead, if they woke in us an image,
look, perhaps they would point to the catkins, hanging
on the bare hazel branch; or else
they would mean the rain falling on earth's dark realm in Spring.

And we who think that happiness
ascends, would feel the emotion
that startles us, almost,
when a stroke of fortune *falls*.

1923 (written 1912/1922)

JOHANN WOLFGANG VON GOETHE

Primal Words. Orphic

ΔΑΙΜΩΝ, DAEMON

As stood the sun to the salute of planets
Upon the day that gave you to the earth,
You grew forthwith, and prospered, in your growing
Heeded the law presiding at your birth.
Sibyls and prophets told it: You must be
None but yourself, from self you cannot flee.
No time there is, no power, can decompose
The minted form that lives and living grows.

ΤΥΧΗ, CHANCE

Strict the limit, yet a drifting, pleasant,
Moves around it, with us, circling us;
You are not long alone, you learn decorum,
And likely act as any manjack does:
It comes and goes, in life, you lose or win,
It is a trinket, toyed with, wearing thin.
Full circle come the years, the end is sighted,
The lamp awaits the flame, to be ignited.

ΕΡΩΣ, LOVE

Love is not absent! Down from heaven swooping,
Whither from ancient emptiness he flew,
This way he flutters, borne by airy feathers,
Round heart and head the day of Springtime through,
Apparently escapes, returns anon,
So sweet and nervous, pain to pleasure gone.
Some hearts away in general loving float,
The noblest, yet, their all to one devote.

ΑΝΑΓΚΗ, NECESSITY

Then back it comes, what in the stars was written;
Law and circumstance; each will is tried,
All willing simply forced, by obligation:
In face of it, the free will's tongue is tied.
Man's heart forswears what most was loved by him,
To iron 'Must' comply both will and whim.
It only seems we're free, years hem us in,
Constraining more than at our origin.

ΕΛΠΙΣ, HOPE

Yet the repulsive gate can be unbolted
Within such bounds, their adamantine wall,
Though it may stand, that gate, like rock for ever;
One being moves, unchecked, ethereal:
From heavy cloud, from fog, from squall of rain
She lifts us to herself, we're winged again,
You know her well, to nowhere she's confined –
A wingbeat – aeons vanish far behind.

1817–18

RAINER MARIA RILKE

Mausoleum

King-heart. Seed of a lofty
monarch-tree. Balm fruit.
Golden heartnut. Urn poppy
in mid-nave's midst
(where the echo ricochets
like a splinter of silence
when you move,
because you feel
your former
posture was over-loud . . .)
drawn away from peoples,
starminded,
in the invisible circle
circling king-heart.

Where is, where is it gone,
that of the light in-
amorata?
: Smile, from without,
laid on the hesitant
curve of calm fruits,
or else a precious thing
of moth, lace wing, feeler . . .

But where, where, that sang them,
sang them to union,
the poet-heart?
: Wind,
invisible,
wind-innermost.

October 1924

211

FRIEDRICH HÖLDERLIN

Patmos

For the Landgrave of Homburg

Near and
Hard to grasp is
                    The God.
But where danger is,
        Deliverance also grows.
The eagles
        Dwell in obscurity
            And across chasms fearless go
                    The sons of the Alps, on bridges
Lightly built. Wherefore,
            Since the peaks of time cluster
            High all around
And loved ones dwell
                    Near, languishing
                On mountains farthest apart,
Give us innocent
                    Water, O give us the wings
With truest mind to travel
            Across and to return.

Thus I spoke
And a spirit
            Rapid beyond my expectation
                    Carried me far
From my own house to where
        I never thought to go.
                    The shadowy forest
Darkened
    In twilight as I went,
And rivers of my native land,
                Yearning; countries there were
I never knew; but soon
                In the first sheen rose
Mysterious in golden haze,
                Rapidly full grown

212

With sunlight's paces, fragrant
    With a thousand peaks

    Asia, across my vision, all in bloom,
And dazzled
      I peered to find
         One thing I knew, being not
Familiar with the spacious lanes down which
      Paktolus travels, tricked
         With gold, from Tmolus,
And where Tauros stands,
            And Messogis, and
The garden, full of flowers,
         A calm fire, but in the light
High up the blush of silver snow
           And, stuff of life immortal
      On walls unapproachable,
    Primordial the ivy grows,
         And borne aloft
By living columns, cedar and laurel,
        The solemn godbuilt palaces.

    But round the gates to Asia
Murmur
        Passing this way and that on the sea's
      Uncertain plain
        Shadowless roads enough, though any
Seafarer knows
      The islands. And since I heard
Patmos was among
      Those near at hand,
    Much I desired to put in there
        And be close
To the dark cave. For not
      In splendour, like Cyprus with
    Its abounding waters, nor
Like any other island
      Does Patmos dwell,

But still hospitable
In her poorer house,
    And if a stranger comes
      From shipwreck or grieving
For his lost homeland or a far friend,
        She listens, and her children,
Voices of the hot thicket,
        A trickle of sand, earth
Splitting in a field, her sounds,
    They hear him and a loving echo
Flows from his lament.
        Thus did she care
Once for the Godbeloved,
    Visionary who, in blessèd youth,

Had walked with the Son of the Highest
And inseparably,
    For the stormbearer loved the simpleness
    Of his disciple, and he, attentive, saw
Plainly the God's face
    When at supper they sat assembled
    And it was the mystery of the vine,
    And the Lord in his great
Soul with calm foreknowing spoke
    Of his death
    And of the ultimate love. For of goodness
He told, more than abundantly, and to bring
    Joy, seeing the fury of the world. For all
Is good. He died
    Thereafter. Much might be said
    Of that. And him they saw, and his
Victorious look, his friends
    Saw him, gladdest at the last.

Yet they were sorrowful, now
As night had begun, and were astonished,
    For great things destined
      They harboured in their souls,
      But life they loved
Under the sun, and wished not to leave

214

The Lord's sight and their native land. It was
Driven deep in, this was,
        Like fire in iron, and the shadow
    Of him they loved walked at their side. So
He sent them the spirit,
        And the house, of course, shook
And God's far storms
            Rumbled over their heads, divining much,
    Now they were gathered, deep
In thought, the heroes of death,

    And in valediction
Again he appeared to them.
        For now the day-sun, royal, he quenched
        And broke the straight
Rayed sceptre, nothing loath, in godly agony,
        For there should be
            Another coming, in good time. Not good
                Would it have been, later, and
Snapping off harshly
        Achievement of men, and joy it was
    To live the present and hereafter
In loving night and keep, steadfast, in simple eyes
            Chasms of wisdom. And deep among
        Foothills also living
                Images break into leafgreen,

    But terrible it is, how infinitely
Far and wide God scatters what lives.
        For even to vanish from the sight
    Of his dear friends and go alone
            Far, over the mountains, when
        The spirit of heaven, doubly known,
Was one in mind; and not
        Foretold it was, but seized them, there
            That very moment
By the hair, when the God fast
            Far off suddenly looked
Back at them, and
        As they begged him

215

Stop, linked as by golden cords,
        Hereafter naming evil, they
Clasped each other's hands –

    But when he dies then
To whom beauty
        Most clung, making his form
Flesh of a miracle
        And the powers of heaven
Pointed to him, and when, eternally
    Riddles to one another, they
        Cannot grasp one another, who
Lived as one
    In memory, and when it takes away
Not the sand only, nor the willows,
        When it takes hold
    Of the temples, when the demigod
And his own are all
        Stript of honour, and even the Highest
Averts his gaze, whence not a shred
    Of immortality is seen in heaven or on
The green earth, what is this?

    It is the cast
Made by the sower when he scoops
        Wheat into the shovel and sweeps it
In an arc
    Toward the clear
        Void over the threshingfloor,
The husk falls at his feet, but
        The grain does reach its goal,
And no bad thing it is, if
        Some disappears, the live sound
    Of speech
        Fades, for divine work too is akin
To ours, the Highest does not want
    All things at once. True,
        The shaft bears iron
        And Etna glowing resins,
So might I have the wherewithal

        To make an image, and see
Christ as he was,

        But suppose someone clapped the spurs
To himself, and on the road
                Morosely talking
            Set upon me, defenceless, much
To my surprise, and it was
                A mere minion trying his hand
                At the image of God – in wrath visible
Once I saw
            The Lord of heaven, not that I
Should be something, but to learn.
                                They are benign
But hate most, as long
            As they are sovereign,
                Falseness which makes
Void the humanity between humans, for
            They do not rule, what rules
Is destiny, of immortals, and their work moves
            In its own motion
                Now speeding to an end.
For when heaven's triumph passes on
            Yet higher, then strong men call
The exultant Son of the Highest,
                Like the sun,

    A beacon, and here is the song's
Staff, pointing downward,
            For nothing is ordinary. It wakes
The dead not caught by crudeness
            Yet. But many
Timorous eyes are waiting still
                To see the light. They want
            Not to flower
                In the sharp ray, although
The golden halter curbs
                Their mettle. But when,
As from brown arched eyebrows,
            Oblivious to the world

Energy ebbs in a glow assuaged
                    From sacred scripture, they
May school themselves, glad of Grace to come,
            In that calm gaze.

    And if the gods of heaven now
Love me well as I believe,
                How much greater is
Their love for you, because
        One thing I know is that the will
            Of the eternal father means
Much to you. In the thundering sky
            His sign is silent. And one
Stands underneath it all
        His life long. For still
Christ is living. But the heroes came,
        His sons, all, and sacred scripture,
From him, and actions
            On earth elucidate, to this hour, the stroke
    Of lightning, in a ceaseless race.
But he is there. For known to him
        Are all his works from the beginning.

    Too long invisible, too long
Honour that flows
    From those heavenly ones. For almost
They have to guide our fingers, and
            There is a force
        Ripping the heart out, with insult. For
Each of the heavenly ones
        Wants sacrifice, but if
One be omitted
        Good never came of it. Earth,
            Our mother, we have served, and
        Latest of all have served
                Unwittingly the sunlight, but
                The Father loves most,
Who rules over all, care

For the firm written character
And sound interpretation of such things
As stand permanent. This end
German song pursues.

1802–3

GÜNTER GRASS

Saturn

In this big house –
from the rats
who know about the drains,
to the pigeons
who know nothing –
I live and suppose much.

Came home late,
opened the house
with my key
and noticed as I hunted for my key
that I needed a key
to enter my own home.

Was quite hungry,
ate a chicken
with my hands
and noticed as I ate the chicken
that I was eating a chicken
which was cold and dead.

Then stooped,
took off both shoes
and noticed as I took off my shoes
that we have to stoop
if we want to take
shoes off.

I lay horizontal,
smoked the cigarette,
and in the darkness was certain
that someone held out his open hand
when I knocked the ashes
from my cigarette.

At night Saturn comes
and holds out his hand.
With my ashes, he
cleans his teeth, Saturn.
We shall climb
into his jaws.

1960

HANS MAGNUS ENZENSBERGER

Ode to Nobody

your smoky heart is witness,
singular king, in the wind
your eye of sorrow.
you are magic's journeyman,
enlightened by many deserts,
by disobedience crowned.
you are not modelled by time,
nor is your loyal brow
bespattered with ash.

you are a spirit without scar,
your sea swell is solemn,
you were before, more perfect
than the great floating rayfish,
anointed, in your glory,
quit of death, king.

but you are not far and early
or late, you are here.
your just glance falls
like snow out of air
and dwells on the wharfs,
passes over observatories
into dusty lost property offices, rests
in wet cement cellars
where the murderers crap, falls
upon thromboses and cannon,
a smacking kiss on slaughterhouses
and tangled refineries
where laughing gas steams, rests
on the intrigues of shipping companies
and skims the comets,
and carcinoma of high finance,
rests on the ramparts of power
behind which substances tick
toward death, and besieges them

till to your throbbing glance
the sky, crusted with mould
of parachutes, falls.

you stride unrecognized,
beauteous squall, by night,
over the spanish square.
your kingdom is restored to you,
hidden one, glass huntsman.

both innocent asparagus and
your image, the brandmarked,
you in your bounty will
despoil and forget.

glory and vengeance are yours,
rock never molested, magic's
journeyman, occult and
singular witness! your windhair,
your bare glance blows across
your ancient kingdom to come,
and in the smoke treasures up,
in the wind, what is true.

1959

PIERRE REVERDY

Heartbeats

One day perhaps the machine will start again under the palm trees
On the sunlit cornice where grindingly the shadow turns
In the dawn of rubbers lost and won far from harbour
When the unballasted ideas are sliding away
In the immense furrow where thirst empties itself
Where the too weightless blood recomposes its waves
When the sea surge rams its shoulder down on the deck
The sailors' song breathing its cadence

To be exact one could count the words
Arrange all the broken features of these faces
On the sky's brow the lines too deeply grooved by effort
And sorrows with difficulty adapted to the shapes of men
One must see these statues of cork on the sea-waves
These disguised forms that squat in the shadow
When the clairvoyant spirit in the flash of some defect
Perceives the implacable future on the tomb's rim

Whoever would think then of return by any other way
Who would dare to climb the calvary steps
One line too many degrades my torment
With a look too faithless the adversary's heart is lost
Not one tear more in mine
Not one precise gesture on the troubled screen of the enigma
Along the endless roads nothing but black markers
And all the time lost in false careers

Yet joy sometimes unfolds its golden branches to the sun's kiss
Love open wide since day's first murmur sheds its petals
Against the pride murdered by your rough hands
The arms thrown stronger and stronger round your neck
At each leap my terrible character makes
These arms that shall be hereafter your loins' wrinkled girdle
Not to be loosened by you not ever
The pitiless force that shall braid our bonds
For all the hurt that you can do to me

1937

ALFRED LICHTENSTEIN

Prophecy

Soon there'll come – the signs are fair –
A death-storm from the distant north.
Stink of corpses everywhere,
Mass assassins marching forth.

The clump of sky in dark eclipse,
Storm-death lifts his clawpaws first.
All the scallywags collapse.
Mimics split and virgins burst.

With a crash a stable falls.
Insects vainly duck their heads.
Handsome homosexuals
Tumble rolling from their beds.

Walls in houses crack and bend.
Fishes rot in every burn.
All things reach a sticky end.
Buses, screeching, overturn.

1913

GEORG TRAKL

Helian

I

In the lonely hours of the spirit,
Beautiful it is to walk in the sun,
Beside the yellow walls of the summer.
Softly the footfalls ring in the grass; but always
The son of Pan sleeps in the grey marble.

Evenings on the terrace we got drunk with brown wine.
Reddish the peach glows in the leaves;
Gentle sonata, happy laughing.

Beautiful is the quiet of the night.
On a dark plain
We meet with shepherds and white stars.

When autumn has come
Sober clearness enters the grove.
Calmed we wander beside red walls
And the round eyes follow the flight of birds.
At nightfall the white water sinks in funeral jars.

In bare branches heaven celebrates.
In pure hands the countryman carries bread and wine
And the fruits ripen peacefully in the sunny larder.

O how earnest is the countenance of the dear dead.
Yet a just regard delights the soul.

II

Immense is the silence of the ravaged garden
When the young novice garlands his temples with brown leaves,
His breath drinks icy gold.

The hands stir the age of bluish waters
Or in the cold night the white cheeks of the sisters.

Soft and harmonious is a walk past friendly rooms,
Where solitude is, and the rustling of the maple tree,
Where still perhaps the thrush is singing.

Beautiful is man and evident in the darkness,
When marvelling he moves his arms and legs
And silent in purple caves the eyes roll.

At vespers the stranger is lost in black November destruction,
Under rotted boughs, beside leprous walls
Where earlier the holy brother walked,
Sunk in the faint thrumming of his madness.

O how lonely the evening wind desists.
Fading, the head bows in the dark of the olive tree.

III

Overwhelming is the generation's decline,
At this hour the eyes of him who gazes
Fill with the gold of his stars.

At nightfall bells die that will chime no more,
The black walls on the square decay,
To prayer the dead soldier calls.

A pale angel
The son steps into the empty house of his fathers.

The sisters have gone far away to white old men,
At night the sleeper found them under the columns in the hall,
Returned from their sorrowful pilgrimages.

Oh how their hair curds with filth and worms
When he plants his silver feet therein,
And from bare rooms they move with dead steps.

O you psalms in fiery midnight rains,
When the servants with nettles thrashed the gentle eyes,
The childlike fruits of the elder tree
Marvelling stoop over an empty grave.

Softly yellowed moons roll
Over the fever sheets of the young man,
Before silence of winter comes.

IV

A high destiny ponders down Kidron passing,
Where the cedar, tender being,
Unfolds beneath the blue brows of the father,
Over the meadow at night a shepherd leads his flock.
Or there are cries in sleep
When in the grove a brazen angel advances on man
And the saint's flesh melts on the glowing grill.

Round the clay huts purple vines abound,
Sonorous sheaves of yellowed corn,
The hum of bees, the flight of the crane,
At nightfall the resurrected meet on mountain paths.

Lepers are mirrored in black waters
Or they part their filth-bespattered robes,
Weeping to the wind that blows with balm from the rosy hill.

Slim girls grope through the alleys of night,
To find the loving shepherd.
On Saturdays quiet singing sounds in the huts.

Let the song also remember the boy,
His madness, and white temples and his departing,
The mouldered boy, who opens bluish his eyes.
O how sorrowful is this meeting again.

V

The stairs of madness in black rooms,
The shadows of the old men under the open door,
When Helian's soul regards itself in the rosy mirror
And snow and leprosy slide from his temples.

On the walls the stars have been extinguished
And the white forms of the light.

From the tapestry bones of the graves descend,
The silence of decayed crosses on the hill,
Sweetness of incense in the purple night wind.

O you crushed eyes in black mouths,
When the grandson in his mind's gentle night,
Lonely, ponders the darker ending,
The quiet god closes his blue eyelids over him.

1913

GÜNTER KUNERT

Fragment

Every life a fragment,
requires a deal of work. These
suspended enterprises. These labours
not undertaken. These defects that persist.
When I consider my person
I see an ant,
it drags a fibre
back and forth and back. You intuit
the magnitude of its readiness
to do its bit, constructing
an exceptional house, but
the rain falls, but
comes overnight a hard freeze
and cancels, perhaps, its precisely reckoned
sum. Even my attention
to it, as to myself, one day
will disperse. We suffer
from a mystery
we thought to be God,
which nobody resolves for us
because we are not able,
ever, to articulate it before
the end, least of all
thereafter.

1996

GOTTFRIED BENN

The Evenings of Certain Lives

I

You needn't always be scrubbing the tiles, Hendrickje,
my eye drinks itself,
drinks itself dry –
but then it has no other liquor –
the statue of Buddha over there,
Chinese god of the bosk,
as against a good tot of Hulstkamp,
I ask you!

Never painted a thing
in frost-white or skater's blue
or in Irish green
with the purple flickering out of it –
only my own monotony always –
my coactive shadows –
it's not pleasant
to follow this bent with such distinctness.

Greatness – where?
I take my pencil
and certain things emerge, stand there
on paper, canvas
or similar things –
result: bronze Buddha as against hooch –
all those obeisances under indoor plants,
banquet of the dimwit daubers' guild – :
give it to the genre painter!

Rattles,
lambs bleating,
transfers,
Flemish, rubenesque,
for small grandchildren –
(likewise idiots – !)

Ah – Hulstkamp –
midpoint of warmth,
centre of colours,
my shadow brown –
aura of unshaved bristle round heart and eye –

II

The fire is smoking
– the Swan of Avon blows his nose –
the tree-stumps are wet,
clammy night, emptiness suffused with draughts –
have done with characters,
earth overpopulated
by copious fall of peach, four rosebuds
pro anno –
strewn far and wide,
thrust on the boards
by this hand,
with its wrinkles now,
and its exhausted veins.

All the Ophelias, Juliets
wreathed, silvery, also murderous –
all the soft mouths, the sighs
I manipulated out of them –
the first actresses long since vapour,
rust, lixiviated, rats' pudding –
even the heart's Ariel off to the elements.

The age takes off its Sunday best.
These duke and desperado skulls,
their trains of thought
I drove to the extreme –
my history-making gentlemen
all illiterates of crown and sceptre,
major powers of space,
like flittermouse or paper kite!

Sir Goon recently wrote to me:
'The rest is silence.'
I think I said that myself,
nobody else could have said it,
Dante dead, – a great emptiness
between the centuries
up to the quotations from my vocabulary –

but if they were missing,
if all that stuff had never been turned out,
the booths and the gallowtrees, if the bells
had never jingled – :
gaps then – ?? Gaps possibly in the teeth,
but the ape's great jaws
would go on grinding
their emptiness the draughts suffuse –
the tree-stumps are wet,
and the butler snores in his porter dreams.

1949

GÜNTER EICH

The Conversation Continues

1. REMEMBERING THE DEAD MAN

I was noticing
that memory is a mode of oblivion.

It meant:
searching for flames in the ash,
geologizing in the rejected
deposits of the instant,
restoring the sequence of time
out of its insoluble chemistry.
It meant:
distinguishing critique of birdflight
from the forenoon shopping
and expectation of love.
Going there
where the parallels intersect.
Through dreams fulfilling
the demands of logic.
Taking the fossils from the glass cases,
to thaw them out with blood warmth.
Searching for the sign
instead of metaphor,
thus for the only place
where you always are.

I get under way
to translate the ant-hill,
taste tea with closed mouth,
slice the tomatoes
under the salt of verses.

2. INVITING HIM IN

The disgrace that the survivor should be right,
relieved of decision making,
with all the arrogance of judgement.

Who will deny
that greenness is green?
That gives our wording
beautiful certainty,
the significance of firm ground.
But the stylization
a heart imposes on itself
contains its motives
like the ammonite
the dead man is looking at.
It would like to put out feelers,
transform vineleaves into fern spirals,
make errors bloom,
hear autumn as the smell of snow.

But don't forget the houses
in which you dwell with us.
The chaise in the garden
will suit you
or the view of trees at the window,
so you can prop your elbows on your knees.
Come in out of the rain and speak!

3. ENTERING INTO CONVERSATION WITH HIM

Here it did not begin and it began,
here it is continued
with a noise in the next room,
with the click of the latch,
with shoes taken off behind the door.
The pallor of your face
becomes invalid, blurred by colours.
Sentences arise from habits
which are hardly noticed.
The manner of knotting a necktie

235

is a conclusive objection,
the ability to fall rapidly asleep
a disproval of one's own explanations,
the preference for tea
arranges the existence of animals.

4. FINDING HIS THEME

Interchangeable
the knock on the door,
with which conversation began,
and the waving
when the streetcar bell rang,
the name on the grave cross
and the name on the garden gate,
children growing up
and greetings on cards from Ragusa.

Words as vibrations of air,
the organ note from the bellows,
the decision
to hear the song
or to be the song, –
slant straight lines
to Phosphor's descendant,
when the theme begins.

No variation tolerated,
not the hedgings of power,
nor the tranquillizations of truth,
with cunning
sniff out the questions
behind the broad back of the answer.

5. READING HIS BOOK AND HIS DEATH

Figures resident
in the shut mineshafts of Zinnwald
behind the demonry
of highland and season,
while the foreground is occupied
by roughnecks who distribute,
among themselves, our moment.

Pirna balanced by the Pyramids,
the freedom of long distance express trains
pocketed as small change by the concierge,
family on an ethical basis,
contempt for nomads and solitaries.

But as eager adjectives
the objections return
into the sentences,
a train of termites
which hollows them out
to a thin skin
of black letters.

Style is the dying,
the bullet in the abdomen,
the white rose in the morphia dream,
the jokes intended, prior to life,
salvoes into the snowstorm.

6. OBTAINING CONFIDENCE FROM HIS LIFE

While you are sharing the thoughts,
guiding the conversation by your death,
also writing the poems,
picking up the pears,
and considering new landscapes
(– but finally I did resist
working in the garden),
all that time Simona froze
becoming a figure of stone,

her imagined warmth
under the chill of the tears.

She is waiting for the moss,
for injuries inflicted by rain,
tendrils and bird dirt.
Weathered, she will be warmed
to a life we wish to share,
patience!

1964

CHRISTOPH MECKEL

Photograph

A woman in a chaise beneath acacia trees
and a glass of wine.
Beauty, unoccupied, clothes loosened in the shade,
Near enough happy, without cause.
Summer raven flocks, dustclouds beyond the walls.

That is what the poem is.
It is what we come through time with, to the end of hope.
It is simple to be right with a few words
and a woman, waiting for the day to end.
A photograph is little, a laugh more, a lifetime not enough.
Memory and Saturn's bones, maybe we need no more,
Near enough deathless in the shade of the trees.

1977

LARS GUSTAFSSON

On All That Glides in the Air

My grave is still nowhere to be seen.
Thus I too glide,
resting, without knowing it.
In an ocean of air
gliding with all that glides,
living with all that lives,
resting with all that rests,
and perhaps, too, not knowing it,
dead with all that's dead.
There is no word for this.
It is a way to glide
'in the ocean of air' as old-fashioned balloonists did,
and this ocean of air is yourself.

Once in Texas at six in the morning,
swimming in the crystal water
of a very deep swimming pool,
intended actually for people who can dive,
my swimming suddenly became a gliding.
Looking down through the small goggle windows
at the marked black and white lanes,
from precisely the height that's fatal if you free-fall,
I could for a moment understand what it is:
to fall continuously, to be inside your fall
and still glide, carried by something invisible.
We see through the old painters and smile at them
and their childish trick of placing
far back in the picture very small birds,
gliding like reckless punctuation marks,
between earth and air, between light and shade,
between water and land, in short
the difference that comes between differences,
the things of twilight that create the depth
which central perspective can't create alone.
So all mortals glide in the interior
of their own picture, somewhere in the twilight,
and for this gliding there is no name.

So also the signs glide over the white pages,
so the rooks glide over the snow, good times
over evil times,
so everything glides, stands as the angels stand
in an unthinkable motion,
and for the flight of the world there is no name.

1984

Coda:

CHRISTOPH MECKEL

Talking about Poetry
  for Christopher Middleton

We have toppled
the tree, have chased
the tree during autumn,
have hung it with hailstones and snow:

we have dried the rivers
and counted the water,
have held the wave up to the light,
and have weighed the flow
in the fountain:

we thought we could capture
the owl, feathers it shed
was all we held, we copied
the owl's talk in our language,
which says: The moon
is a desiccated sun!

World, lost and forgotten
in words a thousand and one –
CHERRYTREE! while the cherrytree flowers
FLOOD! while the sea retreats
on the tracks of the moon –

it is time to stop it
and bring the world home into words,
inhabitable
dream, entrusted to breath, even in sleep
silence reached
along the graveyard lane of language,

Time, to give
cherries to summer, azure
and to let the sea roll over us,
a strong rain

Time, to be silent,
to be, among the things, wordless,
listen, when the world comes near to our house, at night
with the stepping of armadillos,
untranslatable.

1974

Acknowledgements

The translator and publishers gratefully acknowledge permission to include in this book copyright material, as follows:

Adam Yayınları, Istanbul, for poems by Oktay Rifat from *Elifli / Cobanil Şiirler*, 1980, and *Dilsiz ve Çıplak*, 1984; Alianza Editorial, Madrid, for Federico García Lorca's 'Tamar y Amnon' from *Romances gitanos* (1928); Jean Arp und Sophie Taeuber Stiftung, Rolandseck, and Frau Elisabeth Raabe for poems by Hans Arp from *Gesammelte Gedichte I* (1963) and *II* (1974), originally published by Arche Verlag, Zürich; Frau Eva Zahnd-Zollinger and Atlantis Verlag, Zürich, for 'Kloster Fahr' from Albin Zollinger, *Gedichte*, 1956; E.J. Brill, Kinderhook, NY, USA, for the translation of Ibn Khafaja's 'The Mountain Poem', from *The Legacy of Muslim Spain*, ed. Salma Jayyusi, 1992; Haroldo de Campos for the text from his 'Galaxias' in *Xadrez de Estrelas* (São Paulo, Editora Perspectiva, 1976); Jonathan Cape, London, for translations of Georg Trakl from Georg Trakl, *Selected Poems*, 1967; Deutsche Verlags-Anstalt, Stuttgart, for 'Todesfuge' from Paul Celan, *Mohn und Gedächtnis*, 1952; Dumont Buchverlag, Cologne, for texts from Kurt Schwitters, *Das gesamte literarische Werk*, 1973; S. Fischer Verlag, Frankfurt am Main, for the poem by Peter Huchel from his *Chausseen, Chausseen*, 1963; Carl Hanser Verlag, Munich, for texts by Günter Kunert from *Verkündigung des Wetters*, 1966, *Warnung vor Spiegeln*, 1970, *Tagträume* (1965) 1972, *Abtötungsverfahren*, 1980, *Mein Golem*, 1996, and for texts by Oskar Pastior from *Lesungen mit Tinnitus*, 1986, and *Eine kleine Kunstmachine*, 1994; Harcourt, Brace and Company for 'Saturn' from Günter Grass, *In the Egg and Other Poems*; Andreas Okopenko and Verlag Droschl, Graz, for the poem from Okopenko's *Gesammelte Lyrik*; Klett-Cotta Verlag, Stuttgart, for the poems by Gottfried Benn from *Sämtliche Werke: Band I – Gedichte* (edited by Gerhard Schuster in collaboration with Ilse Benn), 1986; Kösel Verlag, Munich, for 'The Unicorn' and 'The Old Woman' from Gertrud Kolmar, *Das lyrische Werk*, 1960; Gerhard Steidl Verlag, Göttingen, for 'Saturn' from Günter Grass, *Gedichte und Kurzprosa / Studienausgabe, Bd. II*, 1994; Christoph Meckel for his poems 'Eine Frau im Liegestuhl' (original title 'Fotografie') and 'Talking about Poetry' (original title in English); Mercure de France, Paris, for 'Les battements du coeur' from Pierre Reverdy, *Main d'oeuvre*, 1949; Natur och Kultur Bokförlaget, Stockholm, for 'The Birds' and 'All That Glides in the Air' from Lars

Gustafsson, *Föglarna*, 1984, for 'Ballad of the Paths in Västmanland' from *Artesianska brunnar kartesianska drömmar*, 1980, and for 'Elegy on the Density of the World' from *Förberedelser för vintersäsongen*, 1990, also New Directions, New York, for 'The Birds' and 'All That Glides in the Air' from Lars Gustafsson, *The Stillness of the World before Bach*, 1983; Heinz Piontek for his poem 'Die Verstreuten' from *Wassermarken*, 1956, revised in *Indianer-Sommer: Ausgewählte Gedichte*, Bergstadt Verlag, Würzburg, 1990; Rowohlt Verlag, Reinbek / Hamburg, for 'Where Are They' from Rolf Dieter Brinkmann, *Westwärts 1, 2*, 1977, and for 'Pearl Harbour Backwards' from Jürgen Theobaldy, *Schwere Erde / Rauch*, 1980; Suhrkamp Verlag, Frankfurt am Main (in this one case also the Heirs of the Bertolt Brecht Estate) for 'Garden in Progress' from Bertolt Brecht, *Gedichte 5: Gedichte und Gedichtfragmente, 1940-1956*, 1993, for 'Ryoanji' and 'The Conversation Continues' from Günter Eich, *Gesammelte Werke, Bd. 1: Die Gedichte, Die Maulwürfe*, 1991, for 'Ode to Nobody' from Hans Magnus Enzensberger, *landes-sprache*, 1960, for 'Alienation through Work' from Karin Kiwus, *Angenommen später*, 1976, for 'From *The Stone Path*' from Oskar Loerke, *Gedichte und Prosa: Die Gedichte*, 1958, for 'Of burdocks', 'Lost and Near', and 'Depression' from Friederike Mayröcker, *Gute Nacht, guten Morgen*, 1982, for 'A Woman's Awe-Inspiring Blouse' from Robert Walser, *Aus dem Bleistiftgebiet*, Bd. 3, and for the translations from Goethe, *Selected Poems* (ed. Christopher Middleton), 1983, now under licence to Princeton University Press; Penguin Books, London, for translations of Peter Huchel, 'Wei Dun and the Old Masters', and of Günter Kunert, 'The Polish Tree' and 'Film Put In Backwards' from *German Writing Today*, 1967, those texts being now copyright Christopher Middleton. Translations via Spanish from Arabic are from *Andalusian Poems*, published by David R. Godine (U.S. copyright only, 1993); for U.K. and Commonwealth © Christopher Middleton and Leticia Garza-Falcón.

Otherwise unattributed translation copyrights, including those for the translations which originally appeared in *Modern German Poetry, 1910-60* (London, Macgibbon & Kee, and New York, Grove Press, 1962), edited by Michael Hamburger and Christopher Middleton, are copyright © Christopher Middleton, 2000.

Every effort has been made to secure permissions; any copyright holders not named above should contact the publishers.

33044

SCOTTISH POETRY LIBRARY
5 Crichton's Close
Edinburgh EH8 8DT
Tel 0131 557 2876